Econimics of
Farm Production and
Management

Econimics of Farm Production and Management

VT Raju MSc (Ag), PhD

Professor and Head
Department of Agricultural Economics, Agricultural College
Andhra Pradesh Agricultural University, Baptala

D Vishnu Shankar Rao MSc (Ag)

Assistant Professor
Agricultural Economics, Agricultural College
Andhra Pradesh Agricultural University, Baptala

Oxford & IBH Publishing Co. Pvt. Ltd.

New Delhi

(A Unit of CBS Publishers & Distributors Pvt Ltd *)*

CBS Publishers & Distributors Pvt Ltd

New Delhi • Bengaluru • Chennai • Kochi • Kolkata • Lucknow • Mumbai
Hyderabad • Jharkhand • Nagpur • Patna • Pune • Uttarakhand

Econimics of Farm Production and Management

ISBN-13: 978-81-204-0423-6
ISBN-10: 81-204-0423-8

© 1990, VT Raju and DVS Rao

CBS Reprint: 2017, 2019, 2020, 2021, **2024**

OXFORD & IBH
New Delhi
(A Unit of CBS Publishers & Distributors Pvt Ltd)

Published by **Satish Kumar Jain** and produced by **Varun Jain** for
CBS Publishers & Distributors Pvt Ltd
4819/XI Prahlad Street, 24 Ansari Road, Daryaganj, New Delhi 110 002, India
Ph: 011-23289259, 23266861
Website: www.cbspd.com
e-mail: delhi@cbspd.com

Corporate Office: 204 FIE, Industrial Area, Patparganj, Delhi 110 092, India
Ph: 011-4934 4934   Fax: 011-4934 4935   e-mail: publishing@cbspd.com;
publicity@cbspd.com

Branches

* **Bengaluru:** Seema House 2975, 17th Cross, KR Road, Banasankari 2nd Stage, Bengaluru 560 070, Karnataka, India
Ph: +91-80-26771678/79   Fax: +91-80-26771680   e-mail: bangalore@cbspd.com
* **Chennai:** 7, Subbaraya Street, Shenoy Nagar, Chennai 600 030, Tamil Nadu, India
Ph: +91-44-26680620, 26681266   Fax: +91-44-42032115   e-mail: chennai@cbspd.com
* **Kochi:** 42/1325, 1326, Power House Road, Opp KSEB, Power House, Ernakulum Kochi 682 018, Kerala, India
Ph: +91-484-4059061-65,67   Fax: +91-484-4059065   e-mail: kochi@cbspd.com
* **Kolkata:** 147, Hind Ceramics Compound, 1st Floor, Nilgunj Road, Belghoria, Kolkata-700056, West Bengal, India
Ph: +033-25633055, 033-25633056   e-mail: kolkata@cbspd.com
* **Lucknow:** Basement, Khushnuma Complex, 7 Meerabai Marg (Behind Jawahar Bhawan), Lucknow-226001, UP India
Ph: +91-522-4000032   e-mail: tiwari.lucknow@cbspd.com
* **Mumbai:** PWD Shed, Gala no 25/26, Ramchandra Bhatt Marg, Next to JJ Hospital Gate no. 2, Opp. Union Bank of India Noorbaug, Mumbai-400009, Maharashtra, India
Ph: 022-66661880/89   e-mail: mumbai@cbspd.com

Representatives

* Hyderabad   0-9885175004   * Jharkhand   0-9811541605   * Nagpur   0-9421945513
* Patna   0-9334159340   * Pune   0-9923910676   * Uttarakhand   0-9716462459

Printed at Chaman Enterprises, Daryaganj, New Delhi, India

Preface

Agricultural production economics and farm management are the two important fields of Agricultural economics. Both these are also applied fields of economics. While in some Universities and Colleges these two are taught separately, in some places they are taught together. Though, some books are available for these two separately, books containing both are scarce and students and teachers are frequently facing problems. Hence, in this book both are covered.

The book is divided into 8 chapters, the first four dealing with production economics and the other four dealing with farm management. The first chapter introduces the production economics, its role in economic systems, basic concepts, definitions, etc. The second chapter covers the production function, laws of returns, etc. Factor-factor relationships and least cost combination of resources are dealt in chapter three. In chapter four, enterprise combinations and optimum product combinations are discussed. The fifth chapter introduces the farm management and the management aspects of the farm business and application of various economic principles are discussed in this chapter and also in sixth chapter. The role of farm records, efficiency measures, depreciation methods, inventory analysis, etc., are discussed with relevant examples in chapter seven. Farm planning and budgeting techniques are presented in chapter eight.

In this book both fundamental and applied aspects are covered with practical approach. The material is presented in easy and simple language with examples and data. Both under-graduate and post-graduate students of Agricultural Universities, students of applied economics of other Universities will find this book ideally suited to their requirements.

V.T. RAJU
D.V.S RAO

Contents

CHAPTER 1

Production Economics

Economics is the science which studies human behaviour as a relation-ship between ends and scarce means which have alternative uses (Rob-ins). The means to satisfy the unending human wants is organising some sort of economic activity, i.e. organisation of production. In this direc-tion, any economic system irrespective of its mode and methods of production has to perform certain functions, viz. (i) to determine what type of goods and services are to be produced, (ii) to organise the production of goods and services to conform to the wishes of the con-sumers, (iii) to distribute the product, (iv) to maintain and increase its production over time, and (v) adjusting consumption to the stock of goods and services available on hand.

In confirmity to the above functions, the economic system has to organise land, human resources (labour) and capital, both at macro and micro levels. During this process, economists tell about the choice of means which allows the attainment of the given end. Before proceeding to the study of the economic principles for the selection of efficient means, the student should be aware of the following basic characteristics of the factors of production.

Production and Factors of Production

Definition: Production is "a process whereby some goods and services called inputs are transformed into other goods and services called output, which in turn creates utilities".

As a result of the production process, two things result: (i) creation of want satisfying goods and services (utility) and (ii) creation of exchange value. Thus production process not only creates utility, but also creates value for the products.

Productive resources required to produce a given product are called factors of production. These are, (a) land, (b) labour (human resources), (c) capital and (d) organisation (enterprise). Some economists classify these factors of production into two basic groups only, i.e. land and labour, because the other two factors of production are not the original factors of production existing in nature and are the creation of human beings.

a) LAND

Land stands for all natural resources which yield an income. It represents those natural resources which are useful and scarce.

   i)   It is nature's gift and fixed in quantity.

   ii)   Geographical supply of land cannot be increased but economic supply can be increased by putting the land under intensive and higher use. Land has no supply price. Price of land prevailing in the market cannot affect its supply.

   iii) It is indestructible and permanent.

   iv) It is immovable and immobile.

   v)   Institution of property exists in land, as it can be divided and sold like any other property.

   vi) Land has enormous variability in its structure and fertility. No two pieces of land are exactly alike.

b) LABOUR

Any work whether manual or mental which is undertaken for a monetary consideration is called labour (labour power or labourer's energy)

   i)   Labour is inseparaole from the human being (labourer) as it is a living thing.

   ii)   Without the aid of labour, no land can be productive.

   iii) Labour does not last and is a highly perishable commodity, in the sense the utilisation of labour cannot be postponed as it has some relationship with time.

   iv) Changes in prices affect labour supply and labour cost. A fall in price (wage) below a certain point may increase the supply in the long run.

   v)   In short run, labour supply cannot be adjusted with demand.

c) CAPITAL

Wealth which is used in producing further wealth, or which yields an income is called capital. Capital is not original factor of production. It is man made. All capital is necessarily wealth, but all wealth is not necessarily capital. For making additions to the stock of capital, savings and investment are necessary.

Characteristics of capital

   i)   Capital is productive.

   ii)   It yields income.

iii) Capital is prospective in the sense that we postpone the present use of it for future in anticipation of reward.

Forms of capital
 i) Fixed capital—land, buildings, etc.
 ii) Working capital—Fertilisers, wages, etc.
 iii) Sunk capital—when capital is used to purchase of highly specialised equipment or machinery, which can be used for only one purpose and cannot be used for other purposes, e.g. purchase of textile machinery, etc.

d) ORGANISATION

The role of organisation or enterprise is co-ordinating and correlating the other factors of production. The entrepreneur organises and supervises the production process. The three chief functions of an organiser or entrepreneur are (i) organising, (ii) risk taking or uncertainty bearing and (iii) innovating.

Forms of organisation
 i) Individual producer
 ii) Partnership
 iii) Joint stock enterprise
 iv) Cooperative enterprise
 v) State enterprise

Characteristics of Modern Production

In earlier days, production used to be consumption oriented, based on self-sufficiency of villages. But in modern times production is market oriented, beyond the boundaries of not only villages but also of countries, with linkages in international market.

1) *Large-scale production:* Increase in population, demand for products and increase in consumption needs of people over the time necessitated large-scale production. As a result the small-scale cottage industries have given place to the use of machines.

2) *Extensive use of machinery:* The need of large-scale production brought in the use of machines to save on time and labour, and they played a dominant role in modern times.

3) *Intensive use of capital:* Business occupation requires capital resources. Without capital, organisation of production process in modern times is impossible. Capital in the form of money has become more

popular in use, which has displaced the barter system, finally leading to the use of credit instruments.

4) *Division of labour and specialisation of functions:* We find a number of production processes and stages of production. Each product in modern times requires a number of factor goods to be consumed in the production of final product. Each factor goods has to be manufactured under specialised labour conditions. This has given rise to division of labour. For example, the construction of building (say, the final product) requires the factor goods like bricks, cement, iron, wood material, etc. And all these factor goods are manufactured under specialised labour conditions. Here the functions of such production process and labour are delineated specifically.

5) *Competition and combination in production and distribution:* Large-scale market oriented production naturally results in enormous output and leads to competition at different levels of marketing to gain more sales and profits over others. To prevent cut-throat competition, amalgamation of competing firms in the form of corporations, trusts and cartels, etc., is an important feature in modern production process.

6) *Monopoly rights over production and resources:* A single firm will have an extensive right in producing and distributing an article.

7) *Joint-stock enterprises:* Any individual can enter any number of enterprises by investing money and purchase of shares, without direct participation in the organisation of production process.

8) *State control and Nationalisation:* In the welfare of the population and economically deprived sections of the society, the state controls the economic system to the advantage of the population: for example, government control in food grains distribution-system, nationalisation of banks, government take-over of sick industries (textiles), etc.

9) *Localisation of industries because of raw materials and comparative advantages:* Due to the establishment of production units near to the sources of raw material, the transportation costs and communication costs can be reduced. Hence most of the industries try to localise the production units in areas where raw material is available.

10) *Production for International Market:* Certain sectors of the economy are organised exclusively for the export markets outside the country, especially the manufacturing industries of the western countries and petroleum products from the Gulf countries.

11) *Advertisement and propaganda:* Because of keen competition, the field of advertising and propaganda of the products has developed as a branch in industrial and business management. The success of the firm

to earn profits depends on the extent of its advertising abilities and propaganda machinery.

12) *Speculative business:* The modern enterprises are more prone to the risk and uncertainty of profits, because of keen competition from other firms and fast changing nature of modern methods of production.

13) *Price and product differentiation:* In modern days, a similar product is manufactured by a number of firms. To make maximum sales and to earn profits better than other firms, each firm makes its product with a little differentiation and fixes its convenient price, marketing the same product in different names.

14) *Unemployment and under-employment:* The large-scale automation and mechanisation has displaced the use of human labour due to economics of large-scale production and time. As a result, a large number of workers were thrown out of employment. Vast number of semi-skilled and unskilled labourers find it difficult to get employment, excepting in manual work.

Nature of Production in Agriculture and Industry — Salient features

Agriculture is characterised by certain peculiarities influenced by natural and sociological environment of its own, which make it substantially different from industry.

1) Agricultural production depends too heavily on seasonal and weather conditions, whereas industrial production is not so dependent on weather conditions except for supplies of certain raw materials from agriculture.

2) Agriculture involves a time-lag from the time of expenditure incurred to the time when returns for such expenditure are obtained.

3) Agricultural production units are small, widely scattered as compared with larger units of industrial production and localised in nature of organisation of producers.

4) Agriculturist has little control over the conditions of production. Hence he cannot plan accurately.

5) Agriculture is an industry of small units, where work is carried on in direct connection with his home and family.

6) Agricultural products are joint products. It is difficult to apportion the costs and income. For example, paddy grain + straw production.

7) Agricultural production is seasonal and consumption is regular. Hence agricultural products have to be stored for longer periods, which create storage problems.

8) Agricultural products are bulky in nature and easily perishable, hence transport and marketing problems exist.

9) Agricultural markets are not regulated and there are too many middle-men in the agricultural market system, whereas in industry distribution channels are well defined and controlled by producers.

10) Agricultural production cannot be offered in a short time, with an increase in demand in the market.

11) The demand for agricultural products is inelastic compared to industrial goods.

12) Agricultural labour is disorganised and it is difficult to measure their work. They have a low bargaining power.

13) Agriculture is primarily concerned with the production of food crops, which are basic necessities of life.

14) Farming is a slow business of low turnover as compared to industry.

15) Agriculture is considered not only a means of livelihood but also a way of life in all the under-developed countries.

16) In agriculture, the law of diminishing returns begins to operate at an earlier stage than in industry.

Nature and Scope of Production Economics

Production economics is concerned with choice in making production patterns and alternative uses of resources to attain the ends or objectives of farmers, farm families, the society or nation within the framework of limited resources.

The relationship between ends and means having alternative uses creates the problem of choice-making. The solution to this problem could be given in terms of what was, what is, what could be, what will be and what should be, among various alternatives for attaining given objectives.

Production economics is concerned with two broad category of decisions in the production process:

1) How to organise resources in order to maximise the production of a single commodity, i.e. choice-making among various alternative ways of using resources.

2) What combination of different commodities to produce?

Approaches to the Study of Production Economics

The scientific approach to the study of production economics involves deduction and induction approaches. Deduction approach employs basic principles and logic in establishing hypotheses and formulating research procedures. Induction approach employs statistical or empirical procedures in testing the hypotheses or models, and formulated in the deductive phase of research.

GOALS OF PRODUCTION ECONOMICS

The goals are two-fold:
a) To provide guidance to individual farmers in using their resources.
b) To facilitate the most efficient use of resources from the standpoint of consuming economy.

Maximisation of the product (profits), minimisation of cost and optimisation of resources are certainly the true goals at the farmer level.

DEFINITION, SCOPE AND SUBJECT MATTER OF AGRICULTURAL PRODUCTION ECONOMICS

Definition: Agricultural production economics is an applied field of science, wherein, the principles of choice are applied to the use of capi ., labour, land and management in farming industry.

Scope: From the study and analysis of farm-firm as an individual production unit, we can indicate the profitable courses of action to be taken by producers. We are able to provide the producer with information, which would be useful in his decisions regarding the resource use. Thereby, the study of farm-firm as an economic unit, we may be able to analyse the conditions that confront the producers and suggest the means by which individual firms can get greater returns of their resource use. The study of firms in agriculture helps us to predict the consequences of changes in economic system, on the individual firms and in turn on the aggregate production in the economy.

Subject matter: As a study of resource efficiency, it is concerned with defining the conditions, under which the ends or objectives of farm managers, farm families and the nation's consumers can be attained to the greatest degree.

It is concerned with productivity, i.e. use of incomes from the production resources. As a study of resource productivity, it deals with: (1) resource use, (2) resource allocation, (3) resource combination, (4) resource management, (5) resource administration and (6) resource efficiency.

Its subject matter includes such topics as combination of farm enterprises, methods of production, size of farms, returns to scale, leasing, production possibilities, farming efficiency, use of credit and capital, risk and uncertainty which effect decision making. In short, the subject matter of agricultural production economics is concerned with how farm resources are used, or should be used. Any agricultural problem, which falls in the field or resource allocation and productivity analysis, is the subject matter of agricultural production economics.

OBJECTIVES OF AGRICULTURAL PRODUCTION ECONOMICS

The main objectives are:

a) To determine and outline the conditions which give the optimum use of land, labour, capital and management in the production of crops and livestock.

b) To determine the extent to which the existing use of resources deviates from optimum use.

c) To analyse the forces, which condition production pattern and resource use.

d) To explain means and methods in getting the optimum use of resources from the existing ones.

RELATIONSHIP TO OTHER FIELDS OF SCIENCE

Agricultural production economics is one of the broadest fields of agricultural economics. The physical sciences such as agronomy, geology, animal husbandry, engineering and forestry have great importance in production economics. They define the production possibilities, from which choices must be made. Production economics is also related to other social sciences. The process of decision making under uncertainty, involves psychology as much as it involves economics. Sociology is necessarily involved in production and resource use pattern, as they are very much influenced by farmers group, community and individuals. The political science specify the limitations which are placed through laws, customs and other expressions of the state and groups.

BASIC PRODUCTION PROBLEMS IN AGRICULTURAL PRODUCTION ECONOMICS

The producer or the manager is faced with five basic production problems, on which they have to make production decisions.

1) *What to produce?* The producer is concerned with what products to be produced, i.e. crops only, or a combination of crops with livestock? If crops only, which crops and in what proportion. It is a product–product problem, i.e. selection of enterprise.

2) *How to produce?* What methods and combinations of resources to use? A factor–factor problem, i.e. least-cost methods of production.

3) *How much to produce?* What level of inputs to apply in production. A factor–product problem, i.e. product mix.

4) *When to buy and sell:* The seasonality of supply conditions in factor market and product market results in variations in the prices. The producer must consider these things in determining when to sell or buy.

5) *Where to buy and sell*: The problems like whether to sell in the village market, or in regulated markets, or other alternative markets, are confronted by the producer. The prices in factor and product markets fluctuates from market to market. The producer must decide whether to involve the transportation and other charges, etc.

Basic Terms and Concepts

PRODUCTION VERSUS PRODUCT

Production is a process of transformation of certain resources or inputs into products, which in turn creates utilities for consumption. Products are the result of the use of resources or services of resources.

RESOURCES AND RESOURCE SERVICES

Resources are the agents or factors used in production process. There are some inputs or resources, which get consumed and transformed into products in the process of production; for example, fertilisers, water, insecticides, etc. There are certain resources of which only services are available, which are transformed into products; for example, labour, implements and machinery, buildings, etc. Resources are classified into: (a) fixed and variable resources and (b) flow and stock resources.

FIXED RESOURCES

The level of some resources such as buildings, machinery, implements, is fixed over planning period, irrespective of the level of enterprises taken up. Fixed resources are limited in quantity and their services cease when they are exhausted; for example, buildings, land, machinery, etc.

VARIABLE RESOURCES

The resources whose uses vary with the level of enterprise, are known as variable resources; for example, fertilisers, seed, feeds, etc. Variable resources can be increased or decreased in their quantity.

All resources are variable in the long run. Some fixed resources however, have a variable use, such as tractor services, bullock power. In the short run, they are deemed fixed as their services cannot be changed over a particular unit of time.

FLOW AND STOCK RESOURCES

Flow Resources: There are some resources, if their services are not used, these cannot be stocked for a future period. Services are forthcoming like a flow, for example, labour, building, etc. If the services of every labourer are not used when its services are available, these will not be available for use at a latter period, because as the flow of another period will still be forthcoming.

Stock Resources: The resources, which are not used in one period of production, can be stored for a latter period; for example, seeds, fertilisers, feeds, etc., are used up entirely in the production process and can be stored for next period or season, if not used.

Some factors of production embody both flow and stock services, such as land and machinery. Tractor is a flow service each year, but is a stock service for over 10 years (life-period of tractor).

FARM-FIRM

The firm is a decision making unit or managerial unit (economic unit) of production. A farm is a firm which combines resources in the production of agricultural products on the lines of a business firm, i.e. profit maximisation. Hence we call a farm a firm.

ECONOMIC UNIT VERSUS TECHNICAL UNIT

The application of inputs or measurement of output relate to a technical unit or an economic unit. Technical unit refers to a single fixed unit in production, for which technical coefficients (returns, output, etc.) are calculated, e.g. an acre of land or a hectare of land, a unit of poultry birds, etc. Economic unit refers to aggregation of resources, for which costs and returns are worked out as a whole (economic returns), e.g. farm holding. It is a production unit under one management and is also known as farm-firm. A farm may be the economic unit under one management, which includes two different technical units in different locations in the form of some acres of land or in the form of animals.

TRANSFORMATION PERIOD

Time required for a resource to be completely transformed into a product is referred to as transformation period or the production period. This period varies with the resources. Some resources are transformed into product in a short time period, others over a longer period of time and still others are never completely transformed. These variations give rise to complexities in decision making.

Production Function

Definition: Production function is a technical and mathematical relationship, describing the manner and extent to which a particular product depends upon the quantities of inputs or services of inputs, used at a given level of technology and in a given period of time.

In other words, the relation between inputs and outputs can be characterised as a production function. That is, the level of output of a particular commodity depends upon the quantities of inputs used for its production.

Therefore, in the production function relationship, output (*Y*) is a function of inputs (*X*) used, given by $Y = f(X)$.

Types of Production Function

Production function is of four types:

1. Continuous function,
2. Dis-continuous function,
3. Short-run function, and
4. Long-run production function.

1) *Continuous function*

The doses or levels of input and output can be split up into small units. Response of yield to different levels of inputs, e.g. fertilisers can be applied to a hectare of land in different quantities ranging from a kilogram up to 100's of kilograms.

2) *Dis-continuous function (Discrete production functions)*

Such a function is obtained for input factors or work units, which are used or done in whole numbers such as one ploughing or a number of ploughings. One can only shift from one point to another.

3) *Short-run production function*

Production function which relates to factors and products where some resources are fixed, can be termed as short-run production function.

4) *Long-run production function*

Those input–|output relations which permit variation in the input of all factors can be termed as long-run production function.

The production function can be expressed in three forms, i.e. in th form of table, geometry (graphic) and algebraic forms.

Tabular Form: A tabular form is as follows:

Fertiliser input (X) (kgs)	Total output (Y) (qtls)
0	4
10	6
20	9
30	15
40	20
50	22

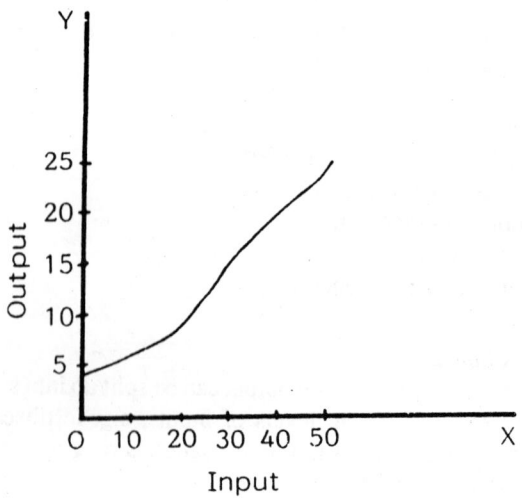

Fig. 1.1. Production function.

Geometrical Expression: The production function also can be expressed by means of a graph, by taking input units on horizontal axis (X axis of the graph) and total output on vertical axis (Y axis) as in Fig. 1.1.

Algebraic form: As an algebraic equation, the Production function is expressed in its general form as $Y = f(X)$, which is read as Y the output is a function of X, the input. Y is a function of X means Y is dependent on X. When more number of resources are involved, i.e. $X_1, X_2, X_3, X_4,$ ..., X_n in the production of a product Y, the equation is expressed as $Y = f(X_1, X_2, X_3, X_4,..., X_n)$, which shows that the output is dependent on or determined by $X_1, X_2, X_3, X_4,..., X_n$ resources used. It can also be expressed as $Y = f(\bar{X}_1, \bar{X}_2, \bar{X}_3, \bar{X}_4,..., \bar{X}_n)$, where the bar indicates which of the resources are variable and which are fixed in quantity. In this case, the Y is a function of $X_1, X_2, X_3, X_4,..., X_n$, but the amounts of $X_3, X_4,...,$ X_n are held constant and X_1, X_2 quantities are varied.

The input–output relationship can be quantified by expressing the algebraic equation as $Y = a + bX$ or $Y = aX^b$, where a is constant (i.e. the amount output Y without any application of X resource), b is the coefficient of X indicating the rate of change in Y as a result of one unit increase in X.

$Y = a + bX$ is a linear equation.

$Y = aX^b$ is an exponential equation (non-linear) and is known as Cobb-Douglas production function.

$Y = a + bX \pm cX^2$ is a quadratic equation.

DEPENDENCE OF PRODUCTION FUNCTION

Production function depends on the following factors:
1) Quantities of resources used
2) Level of technical know-how of the producer
3) Possible methods in production
4) Size of the firm
5) Nature of firms organisation
6) Relative prices and combination of factors of production.

Choice Indicator, Physical and Economic Efficiency Measures, Elasticity of Production

A choice indicator is a yardstick or an index or a criterion indicating which of the two or more alternatives is optimum, or will maximise a given objective or end e.g. price ratios, substitution ratios, etc. It is the criteria used to select between two or more alternatives. For example, a farmer has one unit of a resource for use either in paddy or sugarcane production. He has to choose the application of this resource between these two crops, with an objective of profit maximisation. For example, one unit of resource yields say 40kg of paddy and 100kg of sugarcane. The selection is decided by the price ratios. If the price of paddy is Rs. 2 per kg and sugarcane Rs. 1.50 per kg, the one unit of resource yields, Rs. 80 and Rs. 150 for its use in paddy and sugarcane, respectively. The choice ratio is sugarcane 2/1.5 and obviously the farmer should select sugarcane. The yield ratio is 100/40=2.5/1; the ratio of paddy price to sugarcane price must be greater than 2.5/1 before the resources are used to paddy.

TOTAL PHYSICAL PRODUCT (TPP)

Total output measured in physical terms is called total physical product or total product.

AVERAGE PHYSICAL PRODUCT (APP)

$$\frac{Average\ physical}{product\ (APP)} = \frac{No.\ of\ units\ of\ output}{No.\ of\ units\ of\ input} = \frac{Y}{X}.$$

APP at a particular level of input is measured by dividing the number of units of total product (output) at a particular level, by the number of units of input applied at the corresponding level. It is defined as the ratio of the total product to the quantity of input used in producing that amount of product.

MARGINAL PHYSICAL PRODUCT (MPP)

It is measured as the change in output which results from applying an additional unit of input.

$$Marginal\ physical\ product\ (MPP) = \frac{Additional\ output}{Additional\ input} = \frac{\Delta Y}{\Delta X},$$

where, Δ (delta) means 'change in' or 'addition to' the product/input. It is the ratio between additional output and additional input. It gives the rate of change in output, as the amount of input increases.

ELASTICITY OF PRODUCTION

The production elasticity concept is of greater importance in input-output analysis. It is a measure of responsiveness of output to an increase in input. It is defined as the percentage increase in output as in relation to the percentage increase in input. It is popularly denoted by the symbol E_p.

$$Elasticity = \frac{Percentage\ change\ in\ output}{Percentage\ change\ in\ input} = \frac{\Delta Y}{Y} \times 100 \Big/ \frac{\Delta X}{X} \times 100$$

$$= \frac{\Delta Y}{Y} \times \frac{X}{\Delta X} = \frac{\Delta Y}{\Delta X} \times \frac{X}{Y}$$

These terms can be rearranged as

$$Elasticity = \frac{\Delta Y}{\Delta X} \times \frac{X}{Y} = \frac{\Delta Y}{\Delta X} \Big/ \frac{Y}{X} = \frac{MPP}{APP}$$

Example: Let the application of four (4) units of input give rise to 50 units of output of wheat. If the input is increased by 2 units, the output increases by 10 units. The relative change in input is 2/4=50% and the relative change in output is 10/50=20%. Therefore elasticity of production is 20/50=0.4.

TOTAL VALUE PRODUCT (TVP)

Output measured in monetary term is called total value product. If it is from resource X, it is denoted TVP_x. $TPP_x \times P_y = TVP_x$ (P_y = price of the product).

AVERAGE VALUE PRODUCT (AVP)

It is total value product divided by the amount of resource.

$$\frac{TVP_x}{X} = \text{AVP or APP measured in value terms}$$
$$\text{i.e. } APP \times P_y = AVP.$$

MARGINAL VALUE PRODUCT (MVP)

Marginal product measured in value terms is called marginal value product.

$$MPP \times P_y = MVP \text{ or } \frac{\Delta Y}{\Delta X} \times P_y = MVP.$$

CHAPTER 2

Factor–Product Relationships

There can be three types of input–output relationships in the production of a commodity, where one input is varied and the quantities of all other inputs are fixed. The nature of relationships between a single input and a single output can be either the one or a combination of the types given below.

    a) Law of constant returns (Constant Marginal Productivity).
    b) Law of increasing returns (Increasing Marginal Productivity).
    c) Law of decreasing returns (Decreasing Marginal Productivity).

a) LAW OF CONSTANT RETURNS
    In constant returns, each additional unit of the variable input, when applied to the fixed factor(s) produces an equal amount of additional product, i.e. the amount of product increases by the same magnitude for each additional unit of input.

    This relationship is termed as a linear function and is not very common in agriculture. The production function is a straight line (Fig. 2.1). The output is measured on Y-axis and input on X-axis. The rate of change in output, i.e. Marginal Product for every unit of input is given by the slope of the straight line. At any point on the line, the slope is determined by $\dfrac{\Delta Y}{\Delta X}$. For example the change in Y, i.e. ΔY due to the change in input application from 10 to 15 kg ($\Delta X = 5$) of seed is 2 (Table 2.1). The slope is $2/5 = 0.4$. The slope on this straight line at any point is 0.4. This indicates that for every one unit (5 kg in this case) increase in input, the output increases by 2 units and the average rate of change or average marginal product is 0.4.

    The production function had the same slope throughout its entire range expressed as:

$$\frac{\Delta_{1Y}}{\Delta_{1X}} = \frac{\Delta_{2Y}}{\Delta_{2X}} = \frac{\Delta_{3Y}}{\Delta_{3X}} = \cdots \frac{\Delta_{nY}}{\Delta_{nX}}.$$

b) LAW OF INCREASING RETURNS
    In the law of increasing returns, for each additional or marginal unit

of input results in a larger increase in the product than the preceding unit,
i.e. increasing returns from the input.

Table 2.1. Constant marginal productivity

Seed (X) kg	Output (Y) qtl.	Marginal input (ΔX)	Marginal output (ΔY)	(Marginal productivity) Marginal rate of returns ΔY /ΔX
5	2	5	2	2/5 = 0.4
10	4	5	2	2/5 = 0.4
15	6	5	2	2/5 = 0.4
20	8	5	2	2/5 = 0.4
25	10	5	2	2/5 = 0.4

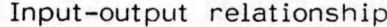

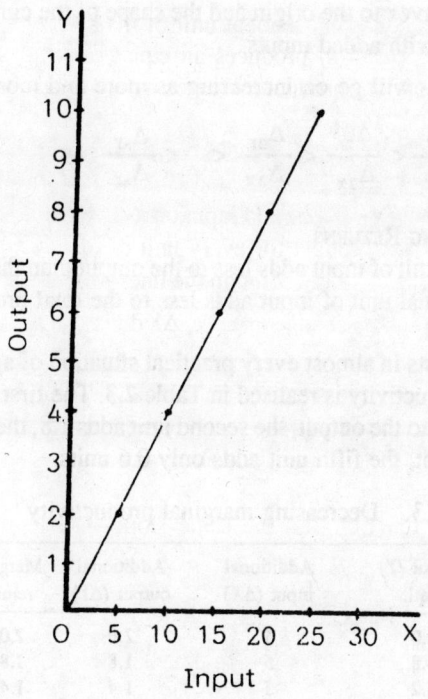

Fig. 2.1. Constant returns to input use.

Each successive units add more to the output than the previous one. The rate of change or the marginal productivity, i.e. $\dfrac{\Delta Y}{\Delta X}$ from each stage changes from 0.40, 0.48, 0.62–0.76 up to 1.34 (Table 2.2), showing an increasing marginal productivity.

Table 2.2. Increasing marginal productivity

Seed (X) kg	Output (Y) qtl.	Additional input ΔX	Additional output ΔY	Marginal rate of returns ΔY/ΔX
5	2.0	5	2.0	2.0/5 = 0.40
10	4.4	5	2.4	2.4/5 = 0.48
15	7.5	5	3.1	3.1/5 = 0.62
20	11.3	5	3.8	3.8/5 = 0.76
25	18.0	5	6.7	6.7/5 = 1.34

If these data can be plotted on a graph (Fig. 2.2), it takes the form of a curve, which is convex to the origin and the shape of the curve will go steeper and steeper with added inputs.

The ratio of $\dfrac{\Delta Y}{\Delta X}$ will go on increasing as more and more units of input are added. $\dfrac{\Delta_{1Y}}{\Delta_{1X}} < \dfrac{\Delta_{2Y}}{\Delta_{2X}} < \dfrac{\Delta_{3Y}}{\Delta_{3X}} < \cdots < \dfrac{\Delta_{nY}}{\Delta_{nX}}$

c) LAW OF DECREASING RETURNS

Each successive unit of input adds less to the output than the previous unit, or each additional unit of input adds less to the total product than the previous unit did.

This function exists in almost every practical situation of agriculture.

Diminishing productivity is realised in Table 2.3. The first input unit (5 kg) adds 2.0 units to the output, the second unit adds 1.8, the third unit adds 1.4 and like that, the fifth unit adds only 0.6 units.

Table 2.3.   Decreasing marginal productivity

Seed (X) kg	Output (Y) qtl.	Additional input (ΔX)	Additional output (ΔY)	Marginal rate of returns ΔY/ΔX
5	2.0	5	2.0	2.0/5 = 0.40
10	3.8	5	1.8	1.8/5 = 0.36
15	5.2	5	1.4	1.4/5 = 0.25
20	6.3	5	1.1	1.1/5 = 0.22
25	6.9	5	0.6	0.6/5 = 0.12

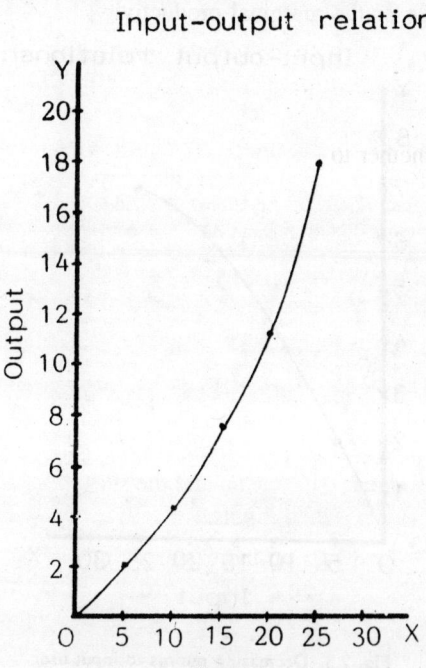

Fig. 2.2. Increasing returns to input use.

If the above relationship is plotted on a graph, the curve will take a form, which is concave to the origin (Fig. 2.3). The productivity of factor decreases progressively as the input level increases, from 0.40 to 0.12.

Elasticity of Production and Production Function

A production with an elasticity of 1.0 ($Ep = 1.0$) throughout indicates constant returns, i.e. one per cent increase in input is always accompanied by one per cent increase in output.

A production function with an elasticity of greater than one ($Ep > 1.0$) throughout indicates increasing returns, i.e. one per cent increase in input is always accompanied by a more than one per cent increase in output.

A production function with an elasticity less than one ($Ep < 1.0$) throughout indicates decreasing returns, i.e. one per cent increase in input always accompanied by less than one per cent increase in output.

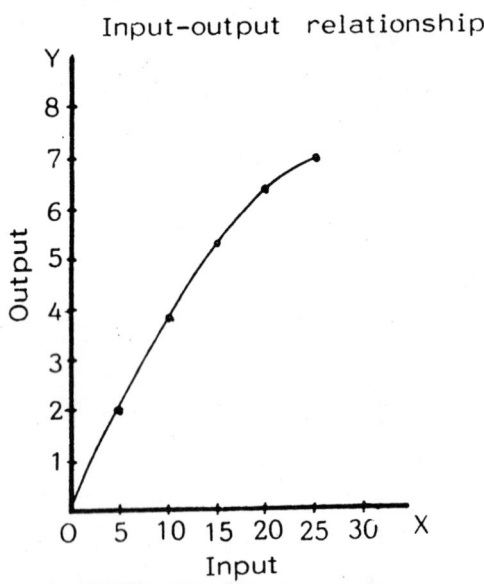

Fig. 2.3. Decreasing returns to input use.

Relationship between Total, Average and Marginal Products

The three basic productivity relationships can be expressed simultaneously by defining the nature of production function (total product curve) in relation to marginal product and average product. The marginal and average product are the derivations from the total product. Hence if we know the total production function, we can arrive at the marginal and average products and establish the relationship among the three physical measures. This relationship was illustrated in Table 2.4 and the respective curves are presented in Fig. 2.4 in its classical way.

The above relationship if plotted on a graph the curve will take the form, which is concave to the origin. The productivity of factor decreases progressively as the input level increases.

SUMMARY OF TP, AP, AND MP RELATIONSHIPS

MPP & TPP

1) When MP increases   = TP increases at increasing rate

2) MP is constant   = TP increases at constant rate
3) MP decreases   = TP increases at decreasing rate
4) MP is zero   = TP is maximum
5) MP is below zero and
   negative   = TP decreases at increasing rate
6) MP is maximum   = Inflection point on TP curve

APP & TPP
1) When MP > AP   = AP is increasing
2) When MP < AP   = AP is decreasing
3) MP equals AP   = AP is at maximum

Table 2.4. Relationship between total, average and marginal products

Fertiliser input (X)	Total product (Y)	Change in input ΔX	Change in total product ΔY	Average product Y/X	Marginal product $\Delta Y/\Delta X$	Remarks
0	0	1	—	0	—	Total product
1	2	1	2	1	2	Increasing at
2	6	1	4	3	4	Increasing rate
3	11	1	5	3.60	5	
4	17	1	6	4.25	6	Increasing at
5	23	1	6	4.60	6	constant rate
6	27	1	4	4.50	4	Increasing at
7	30	1	3	4.28	3	decreasing
8	32	1	2	4.00	2	rate
9	33	1	1	3.66	1	
10	33	1	0	3.30	−1	
11	32	1	−1	2.91	−1	Decreasing at
12	29	1	−3	2.41	−3	increasing rate

Relationship between Total Product and Marginal Product

1) When total produce (TP) is increasing, the marginal product (MP) is positive throughout its range.

2) When TP is at its maximum, MP will be zero.

3) If TP starts decreasing at an increasing rate, MP will be negative.

4) As long as MP moves in upward direction or increases, TP increases at an increasing rate.

5) When MP remains constant, the TP increases at a constant rate.

6) When MP starts or declining slopes downwards, the TP increases at a decreasing rate.

7) At the point of MP = 0, or if MP curve crosses x-axis, the TP will be at maximum.

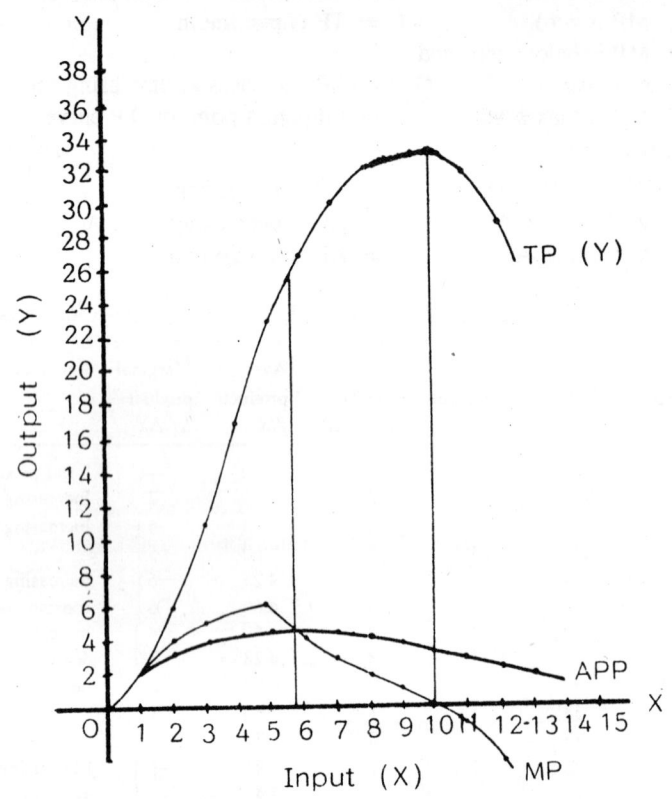

Fig. 2.4. Law of variable proportions—relationship between total product, marginal product and average product.

Marginal Product (MP) and Average Product (AP) Relationship

1) When MP keeps increasing or in moving upward from the beginning, the AP curve also keeps moving upward, below the MP curve.

2) As long as MP curve remains above AP curve, AP curve keeps increasing.

3) When MP curve is below AP curve, APP starts declining and the marginal product is less than average product.

4) If APP does not change with additional input used, the marginal output is equal to APP. APP = MPP.

5) When average product is maximum, here MP equals to AP and from here onwards AP will start to decline. MPC is less than APC, the MP curve must therefore intersect APP from above at its highest point, because at this point both are equal and change from greater to less.

Law of Variable Proportions or Law of Diminishing Returns

Definitions

1) "If the quantity of one productive service is increased by equal increments, with the quantity of other resource services held constant, the increments to total product may increase at first but will decrease, after a certain point" (E.O. Heady).

2) "An increase in capital and labour applied in the cultivation of land causes in general, less than proportionate increase in the amount of product raised, unless it happens to coincide with an improvement in the arts of agriculture" (Marshal)

In other words, as the amount of a variable resource used in the production of a product is increased, the output of the product will at first increase at an increasing rate, then increase at a decreasing rate and finally a point will be reached, where further applications of the variable resource will result in a decline in the total output of the production. In short, the marginal physical product of variable resource will first increase, then decrease and finally become negative. This point in fact is the maximum point on the marginal product curve.

Three Stages of Production Function

The input–output relationship showing total, average and marginal productivity can be divided into three regions in such a manner, that one can locate the portion of the production function, in which the production decisions are rational. The stage I extends from zero input to fifth input level of variable factor, which otherwise ends when maximum point on the average curve is reached. Stage 2 ranges from this point of maximum average product to the point of maximum total product, i.e. fifth input level to ninth input. Stage 3 extends from the zero marginal product to over the entire range of declining total product, i.e. all inputs greater than ninth one, which results in declining total product in the figure.

Stage 1

Characteristics

1) This stage starts from the point of origin up to the point where MPP remains greater than APP.

2) APP increases through this region, indicating the efficiency of all the inputs, if the variable input keeps increasing.

3) TPP increases with increasing rate

4) Stage I ends when APP is maximum or MPP = APP.

5) Elasticity of production (Ep) is more than unity, because MPP is greater than APP, up to maximum average product. At maximum average product, Ep is one.

6) *Point of inflection:* Point of inflection occurs in stage I, where the rate of increase in output start to fall off and the production function becomes concave downwards. When MPP is maximum, the corresponding point on TPC is called point of inflection. Inflection point indicates the change in curvature of TPC.

STAGE 2

1) This stage is obtained when MPP is decreasing and is less than APP. i.e. APP > MPP.

2) Ends when TPP is maximum and MPP is zero.

3) At starting point of this stage MPP = APP where Ep is one.

4) TPP increases at decreasing rate.

5) Optimum point of input use is in this rational region. This region embodies diminishing phase region.

6) If the producer want to maximise their profits, he must operate in Region 2 of production function.

7) Elasticity of production is less than one, but greater than zero between maximum average product and maximum total product.

STAGE 3

1) TPP decreases.

2) MPP crosses zero point and becomes negative.

3) TPP also decreases but it is still positive.

4) It is not a profitable zone, additional quantity of input reduces TPP.

5) Ep is less than zero as total product declines.

6) Double loss—Irrational zone
   a) Reduced production.
   b) Unnecessary additional cost of inputs.

Graph: The figure 2.4 shows the production function with its derived MPP and APP curves. So long as TP rises at an increasing rate, MPP also increases and the production function is concave upwards. At point A, TPP starts to increase at a diminishing rate, MPP starts to decrease and the production function becomes concave downwards. TPP is maximum at *B*, and at this level of output MPP value becomes zero. After this, if more of the variable factor is applied TPP will fall absolutely, in which case MPP becomes negative.

So long as MPP increases, APP will also increase. It will continue to do so eventhough MPP starts to fall, so long as MPP is greater than APP. From *A*, the point of inflection MPP decreases and the MPP curve intersects the APP curve at *D*, the point of maximum value of APP. This intersection indicates the equality of MPP and APP at maximum APP.

Irrational and Rational Stages of Production

Irrational production exists if there is any possibility for the rearrangement of input levels, either to get a greater product from the same level of resources or to get the same product with smaller outlay of resource levels. Irrational production also exists due to employment of inefficient technique, which does not permit the greater output as above.

Stages 1 and 3 are considered irrational stages of production. In stage 1 the average productivity of variable resources keep increasing and profit can always be increased. Instead of reducing the application of variable resources to fixed factors in stage 1, the farmers can always obtain more product and profits from the same resources. In stage 3, the average product decreases further, marginal product becomes negative and total product is decreasing, showing inefficient use of resources.

Therefore the farmer should prepare between the points of maximum average product and zero marginal product (maximum total product), where the *Ep* is greater than zero and less than one. Within the limits of these points stage 2 is considered. The optimum level of resource use must fall in this region of economic relevance. The optimum point of resource use or the profit maximising amount of product can be decided only with the help of choice indicators, i.e. factor-product prices.

LIMITATIONS OF THE LAW

1) *Improved methods of cultivation:* New techniques of crop production, i.e. improved seeds, crop rotations, modern implements, chemical fertilisers and extension of irrigation facilities, etc., bring in increasing returns. But when these techniques reach saturation without further improvements, the law must operate.

2) *New Soils:* When a virgin soil is brought under cultivation, the additional return for each successive dose of labour and capital may increase for a time in the beginning.

3) *Insufficient capital:* Under limited capital conditions, sometimes

the farmers operate in state 1 a gradual increase in capital application from insufficient application yield more than proportionate return. Later, the decreasing marginal return sets in.

These are the exceptions to the law of diminishing returns.

Profit Maximising Criteria

The two methods of defining maximum profits are (i) Profit from the use of factor is maximised when the marginal product is equated to the price ratio. In other words the optimum quantity of input is a function of factor and product price. (ii) Profits are maximised for the fixed unit if the marginal value productivity of factor is equal to marginal cost of the factor.

Profits are maximum when:

(i) Marginal product = Factor-product price ratio

$$\frac{\Delta Y}{\Delta X} = \frac{P_x}{P_y} \qquad \qquad \ldots \ldots (1)$$

(ii) Marginal cost (MC) = Marginal revenue (MR).

Both (i) and (ii) are identical.

From Eq. (1), we can derive the following equation [Eq.(2)], which states that value of the added output is equal to the value of added input.

$$(\Delta y) \cdot (P_y) = (\Delta x) \cdot (P_x) \qquad \qquad \ldots \ldots (2)$$

Value of added output = value of added input.

When the price of output increases or the input price decreases, the optimum level of input increases. Conversely, if the output price decreases or the input price increases, the optimum level of input decreases. In other words when $\Delta y \cdot P_y < \Delta X \cdot P_x$, the input use should be decreased and, when $\Delta y \cdot P_y > \Delta X \cdot P_x$, the input level can be increased till $\Delta_y \cdot P_y = \Delta X \cdot P_x$, provided the farmer has sufficient capital to use the resources.

The marginal cost of an increment of output is determined by dividing the addition to total cost from using one more unit of resource, i.e. ΔX. P_x divided by increase in output.

$$\therefore \frac{\Delta X \cdot P_x}{\Delta Y} = MC \qquad \qquad \ldots \ldots (3)$$

$$\frac{\Delta Y \cdot P_y}{\Delta X} = MR \cdot$$

From Eq. (1) we can derive Eq. (4) as follows:

$$\frac{\Delta X \cdot P_x}{Y} = P_y \qquad \dots \dots (4)$$

i.e marginal cost is equal to the selling price of the product, or

$$\frac{\Delta Y \cdot P_x}{Y} = P_x \qquad \dots \dots (5)$$

i.e. marginal value product is equal to factor cost.

Most Profitable Level of Production (Optimum Level of Resource Use)

The question of determining the most profitable level of production and the optimum level of factor use is closely linked with their respective prices. The optimum level is defined as that level, which gives the maximum profit from the resource use, i.e. maximum margin of total returns over total costs, or the level where the value of added output is equal to value of added input [Eq. (2) above].

In the following table the physical relationship and economic relationships were presented.

The marginal products for various levels of nitrogen input use in paddy production was presented in Col. 5 of Table 2.5. The marginal costs were calculated by multiplying the marginal input with the price of nitrogen at the rate of Rs. 4.02 per kg and marginal returns were derived by multiplying marginal product with the price of the product at the rate of Re 0.84 per kg of paddy. The total returns and total costs columns were derived by multiplying the respective input-output combinations of Cols. 1 and 2 with their respective prices. The net revenue was the difference between total costs and total returns.

Considering the price of paddy at Rs. 0.84/kg and that of nitrogen fertiliser at Rs. 4.02/kg, the first dose of 10 kg of nitrogen costing Rs. 40.2 yields marginal returns worth Rs. 177.24. Applying second dose of nitrogen brings marginal returns of Rs. 135.24, whereas the marginal cost is only Rs. 40.2. Thus second dose is also profitable. Likewise, the application of nitrogen input can be increased up to 40 kg/ha, where the marginal returns are more than marginal cost, i.e. Rs. 48.72 and Rs. 40.2 respectively. After this, when the fifth dose, i.e. 50 kg of N was applied the MR are only Rs. 5.04, whereas MC is Rs. 40.2. This added cost more than the added returns, which is not profitable. Therefore, the most profitable level of nitrogen application in this case is 40 kg/ha. Beyond this it is not profitable to add more fertilizer. Here at this point, the marginal product is above the factor-product price ratio, i.e. $\frac{\Delta Y}{\Delta X}$

Table 2.5.Physical and Economic efficiency of Resource Application

Nitrogen input (kg/ha) (X)	Estimated yield of rice (kg/ha) (Y)	Additional input (ΔX)	Additional output (ΔY)	Marginal productivity (Δy/Δx)	Marginal cost (MC)	Total cost (TC)	Total returns (TR)	Marginal returns (MR)	Net returns (NR)
0	4437					—	3727.08		3727.08
10	4748	10	211	21.1	40.2	40.20	3904.32	177.24	3864.30
20	4809	10	161	16.9	40.2	80.40	4039.56	135.24	3959.16
30	4918	10	109	10.9	40.2	120.60	4131.12	91.56	4010.52
40	4976	10	58	5.8	40.2	160.80	4179.84	48.72	4019.04
50	4982	10	6	0.6	40.2	200.1C	4187.40	5.04	3987.30
60	4937	10	-45	-4.5	40.2	240.12	4147.08	-37.8	3906.96
70	4842	10	-95	-9.5	40.2	280.14	4067.28	-79.8	3787.14
80	4695	10	-147	-14.7	40.2	320.16	4943.80	-123.48	3623.64

40 kg N is 5.8 and the $\frac{P_x}{P_y}$ is $\frac{4.02}{0.84} = 4.79$.

Beyond 40kg N, the MP is far below the price ratios, hence the farmer should operate at 40 kg nitrogen use by producing 4969 kg of paddy, when the price of paddy is Rs .0.84 and price of nitrogen is Rs. 4.02.

To summarise, a farmer can increase the dose of variable input, as long as the marginal returns are greater than marginal costs and can stop at a point where the MR = MC, or marginal product = factor-product price ratio. This is the optimum level of input to be used.

What is Technology?

Technology is the knowledge applied by man to improve production or marketing process.

EFFECTS OF NEW TECHNOLOGY

Technology, has the effect of raising the production function, i.e producing more product per unit of input. This means that more to l output can be produced by or from inputs that were used prior to the technological innovation, or the same amount of total output can be produced with fewer resources. An example of improvement in technology is presented in Table 2.6.

Table 2.6.Mean grain yield of *Rabi sorghum* (g/ha) as effected by crop residues and nitrogen levels

Technique	N_0	N_{40}	N_{80}
1. Greengram	27.8	40.3	49.5
2. Blackgram	17.2	32.4	47.4
3. Cowpea	19.6	36.0	51.1
4. French bean	24.3	37.5	54.4
5. Finger millet	9.1	25.6	40.95
6. Fallow	27.5	35.7	50.4

Source: G. Bheemaiah *et al.* (1986) Studies on the effect of different crop residues and nitrogen levels on *Rabi* sorghum. *Andhra agric. J.* 33 (2): 142–145.

The data from the technique of applying nitrogen at 80 kg/ha is superior over zero nitrogen or 40 kg of N/ha, because N_{80} yields higher output over the other two techniques of sorghum production. Similarly, the technique of growing sorghum with N_{80} after French bean is superior over other forms of growing sorghum. When no cost differences are involved between these techniques of growing sorghum with N_{80} after the crops shown in the table, a cultivator should choose the technique of

French bean *kharif* and sorghum *rabi* with N at 80 kg/ha, which gives the greater output for any given input levels.

Figure 2.5 shows that the production functions are at higher levels for techniques of higher output levels, say for example, the production function of sorghum after French bean is at higher level over that of cowpea, and for other crops the sorghum production function will be still lower due to low yield techniques.

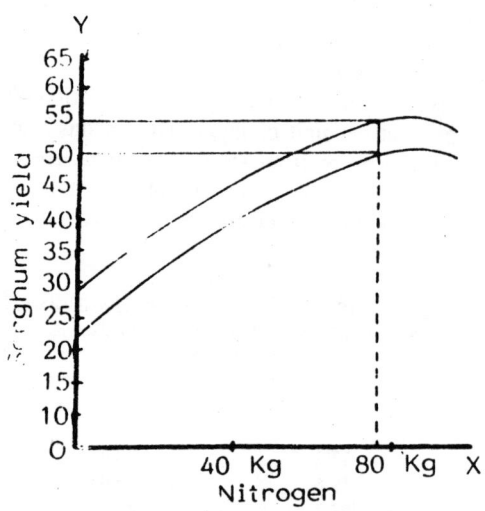

F. 2.5. Improvement in technology and output.

These effects are quantitative. Sometimes qualitative changes are included in the new products technology, which changes the production function. The technological change may call for increased use of certain factors, because of a more complex production technique. For a farm-firm, such technological advances result in:

1) Factor saving technology or cost reducing technology, such as development of improved tractors and machines.

2) Yield increasing technology—HYV and hybrid varieties.

3) Both factor saving and yield increasing technology, either of these

technology developments bring about shifts in the whole body of production function and farmers will face new series of decisions to be taken.

Technological changes can cause:

1) Old products to be replaced by new ones.
2) Create new inputs or improve old ones.
3) Otherwise effect production process.

Production Costs and Their Relationships

In line with the lengths of planning periods, there are two major categories of costs, i.e. fixed costs and variable costs. Fixed costs are those which would be incurred even if no output were produced and variable costs are those costs, incurred only if production is carried on. Variable costs are the relevant costs in making production decisions and the fixed costs have no bearing on production decisions, once they are incurred. To consider whether a particular cost item is a fixed cost or a variable cost, it is to be considered, whether the input is fixed or a variable. In the long run period, all inputs are variable and hence there are no fixed costs.

Table 2.7. Cost Relationships

Output (Y)	Variable costs @ Rs. 10 per unit	Fixed costs @ Rs.40 per unit	Total cost (VC+FC) Rs.	Average variable costs (VC + Y) (Col.2 + Col. 1)	Average fixed costs (FC + Y) (Col.3 + Col. 1)	Average total costs (TC + Y) (Col.4 + Col. 1)	Marginal cost (ΔVC + Y)
0	0	40	40	—	—	—	—
10	10	40	50	1.00	4.00	5.00	1.00
28	20	40	60	0.71	1.43	2.14	0.55
42	30	40	70	0.71	0.95	1.67	0.71
52	40	40	80	0.71	0.77	1.54	1.00
60	50	40	90	0.77	0.67	1.33	1.25
66	60	40	100	0.83	0.61	1.36	1.67
70	70	40	110	0.91	0.57	1.51	2.50
75	80	40	120	1.11	0.55	1.67	5.00

1) TOTAL COSTS (TC)

Total costs are the sum of total variable costs and total fixed costs.

2) TOTAL VARIABLE COSTS (TVC)

These are also called out of pocket costs. The total variable cost represent the sum of expenditure on variable inputs for any level of output. They are short-run costs. Because the farmer has control of all the variable inputs, TVC must be covered in the short-run, or else the farmer will not incur expenditure on these variable inputs.

3) TOTAL FIXED COSTS (TFC)

Sum of expenditures which will be incurred irrespective of output level. These are relatively long-run costs.

4) MARGINAL COSTS (MC)

Marginal cost is the additional cost necessary to produce one more unit of output. Marginal costs depend entirely upon the nature of production function and the unit costs of the variable inputs. Marginal cost is comprised entirely of variable costs. No fixed costs are part of marginal costs, because they are neither increased nor decreased by additional production.

5) AVERAGE VARIABLE COSTS (AVC)

Average variable cost is worked out by dividing total variable costs by the amount of output. AVC varies with the level of production. AVC is inversely related to average physical product, i.e. when APP is increasing, AVC is decreasing, when APP is maximum AVC is minimum.

   i) When AVC is decreasing, the efficiency of the variable input is increasing.

   ii) The efficiency is at maximum when AVC is at a minimum.

   iii) The minimum efficiency is decreasing when AVC is increasing.

6) AVERAGE FIXED COSTS (AFC)

It is worked out by dividing total fixed costs by the amount of output. As output increases, AFC decreases.

7) AVERAGE TOTAL COST (ATC)

It can be computed by two ways: (a) By dividing the total costs by output, or (b) by adding AFC and AVC. The shape of ATC depends upon the shape of the production function. ATC is often referred as the unit cost of production, the cost of producing one unit of output. ATC decreases as output increases.

    1) TC   = TFC + TVC
    2) ATC   = TC + No. of output units (or AFC + AVC)
    3) TFC   = Sum of fixed costs

4) AFC = TFC + No. of output units
5) TVC = TC — TFC, or sum of all variable costs
6) AVC = TVC + No. of output units
7) MC = $\dfrac{\text{Change in total cost or TVC}}{\text{Marginal physical product (MPP)}}$

Algebraic Relationship Among Different Costs

In the production function of $Y = f(X_1/X_2 \ X_3 \dots X_n)$, Y is a function of X_1 and other variables $X_1 \ X_2 \ X_3 \dots X_n$ are held constant at a desired level. The various costs of production may be expressed algebraically as follows; where $P_{x_1} X_1$ is the variable cost and $(P_{x_2} X_2 + P_{x_3} X_3 + \dots + P_{x_n} X_n)$ refers to fixed costs:

$$TC = TVC + TFC$$

$$TVC = P_{x_1} X_1$$

$$TFC = \sum_{j=i}^{n} P_{x_j} X_j \ (j = 2, 3, \dots, n)$$

$$ATC = \frac{TVC + TFC}{Y} = AVC + AFC$$

$$AVC = \frac{TVC}{Y} = \frac{P_{x_1} X_1}{Y} = P_{x_1} \frac{1}{APP_{x_1}}$$

$$AFC = \frac{TFC}{Y} = \frac{\sum_{j=2}^{n} P_{x_j} x_i}{Y}$$

$$MC = \frac{d(TC)}{dy} = \frac{d(TVC + TFC)}{dy}$$

$$= \frac{d(TVC)}{dy} + \frac{d(TFC)}{dy}$$

$$= \frac{dP_{x_1} X_1}{dy} + \frac{d(TFC)}{dy}$$

$$= \frac{dP_{x_1} X_1}{dy} + 0$$

$$= P_{x_i} \cdot \frac{1}{MPP_{x_1}}.$$

PER UNIT COST CURVES

In Price and output analysis, per unit cost curves are used extensively, more than the total cost curves. Per unit cost curves show the same kind of information, but in a different form. The per unit cost curves are AFC curve, AVC curve, AC curve and MC curve.

Total cost of a given output is the sum of total fixed costs and total variable costs. As far as the total fixed cost is concerned, it remains constant for all units of output, but we have to incur variable costs, when output increases. Total variable cost is zero when output is zero and increases with increase in output. At first it increase rapidly, but then due to economics of larger production, it does not increase as fast as before, though it jumps up rapidly at a later stage due to diseconomies that set in.

In Fig. 2.6 ST is the total cost curve and it includes the total fixed cost (SS) and total variable cost represented by difference between (SS and ST curves). Average cost per unit is the total cost divided by the number of units produced. It is the sum of the average fixed cost and the average variable cost.

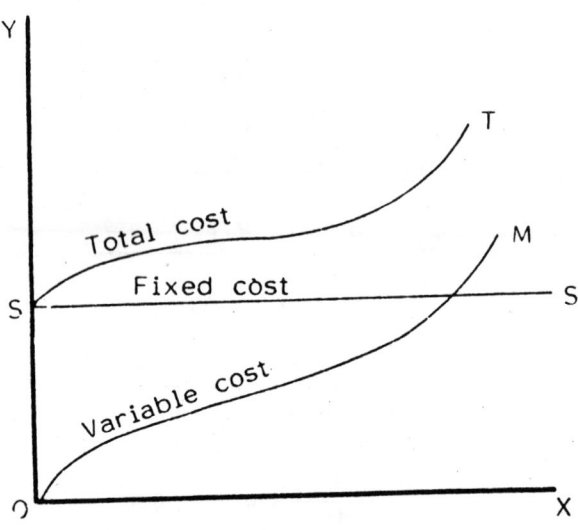

Fig. 2.6. Total, fixed and variable cost curves.

In Fig. 2.7 we have drawn both the average fixed cost curve and average variable cost curve. The total fixed cost being fixed for all units of output, average fixed cost is falling in the shape of a rectangular hyperbola. Average variable cost curve (AVC) at first falls and then rises, as there emerge the diseconomies of large production.

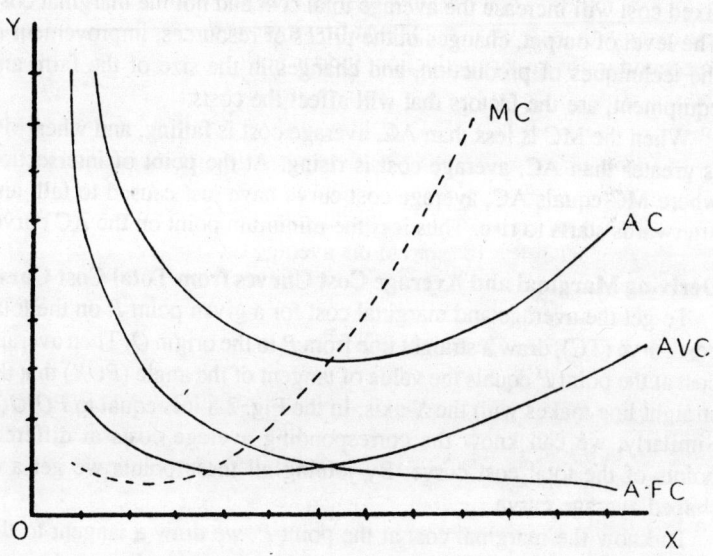

Fig. 2.7. Average and marginal cost curves.

By adding the two costs, average fixed and average variable, we get the average cost (AC) per unit of output. At first average cost is high due to large fixed cost and small output. As output increases, the fixed cost is thinly spread over the larger number of units produced, and the average cost accordingly falls. When diminishing returns set in the variable costs, the average costs start increasing. The lower end of the curve turns up and gives it a U shape.

Marginal cost is the addition to total cost caused by a small increment in output. Marginal cost curve also falls at first due to more efficient use of variable factors as output increases, and then it slopes upward as further additions to the output interfere with the most efficient use of variable factors.

Relation Between Marginal and Average Costs

Average variable cost continues to decline as long as the marginal cost is below it, but it starts rising at the point where MC crosses AVC. MC always rise more sharply than the AVC curve. Similar relation holds between marginal cost and average cost. An increase in variable costs will increase the marginal cost and average total cost. But increase in fixed cost will increase the average total cost and not the marginal cost. The level of output, changes in the prices of resources, improvement in the techniques of production, and changes in the size of the farm and equipment, are the factors that will affect the costs.

When the MC is less than AC, average cost is falling, and when MC is greater than AC, average cost is rising. At the point of intersection where MC equals AC, average cost curve have just caused to fall, and afterwards starts to rise. Thus it is the minimum point on the AC curve.

Deriving Marginal and Average Cost Curves from Total Cost Curve

To get the average and marginal cost for a given point P on the total cost curve (TC), draw a straight line from P to the origin O. Then average cost at the point P equals the value of tangent of the angle (POX) that the straight line makes with the X-axis. In the Fig. 2.8 it is equal to PQ/OQ. Similarly, we can know the corresponding average costs at different points of the total cost curve. By joining all these points we get a U shaped average curve.

To know the marginal cost at the point P, we draw a tangent to the curve TC at the point P. Then marginal cost corresponding to the total cost at P is given by the value of the tangent of the angle that RP makes with the X-axis. In this case it is equal to the value of the tangent of angle PRQ and this equals PQ/RQ, which is the same thing as PM/LM. Similarly, we can know the marginal cost at different points of the total cost curve.

TOTAL COST FUNCTION

A cost function expresses the relationship between cost and output and is determined by factor prices and production function. Cost functions are, (i) short-run cost function and (ii) long-run cost function. In short-run cost function, some inputs are fixed in amount and production is increased only by varying the quantities of other inputs. In the long-run cost function, all the costs of the farm become variable.

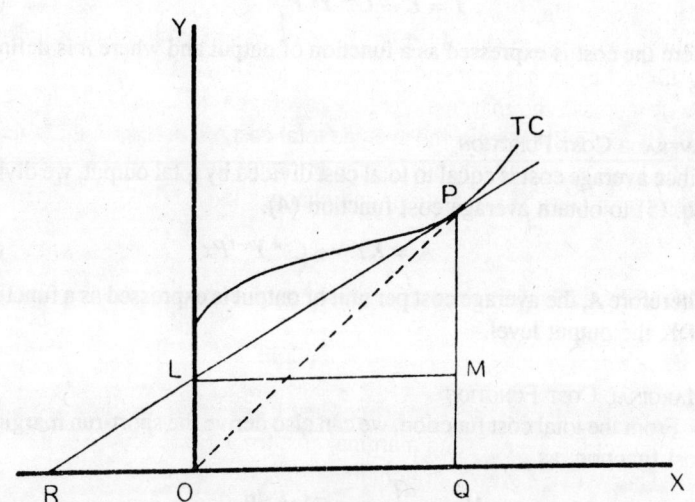

Fig. 2.8. Derivation of AC-MC curves from total cost curves.

When a single resource is variable, the relationship between production function and cost function can be derived as follows:
Production function is given by the following equation:

$$Y = aX_1^{b_1} \cdot X_2^{b_2} \qquad \dots \dots (1)$$

Suppose, X_2 is fixed at some level and therefore $aX_2^{b_2}$ is a constant which is equal to C.

Then Eq. (1) can be expressed as

$$Y = CX_1^{b_1} \qquad \dots \dots (2)$$

From Eq. (2) we can derive Eq. (3) as

$$X = C^{\frac{1}{b}} Y^{\frac{1}{b}} \qquad \dots \dots (3)$$

which indicates the amount of X required to produce a specified level of output Y. Now total cost (T) is the sum of fixed costs K plus the product of the per unit price of factors (P_x) and the quantity of X.

$$\therefore T = K + P_x X \qquad \qquad \cdots \cdots \text{(4)}$$

Substituting the value of X from Eq. (3) for the value of X in Eq. (4), we obtain the short-run total cost function as in Eq. (5)

$$T = K + C^{-n} Y^n P_x \qquad \qquad \cdots \cdots \text{(5)}$$

Here the cost is expressed as a function of output and where n is defined as $\frac{1}{b}$.

AVERAGE COST FUNCTION

Since average cost is equal to total cost divided by total output, we divide Eq. (5) to obtain average cost function (A).

$$A = KY^{-1} + C^{-n} Y^{n-1} Px \qquad \qquad \cdots \cdots \text{(6)}$$

Therefore A, the average cost per unit of output is expressed as a function of Y, the output level.

MARGINAL COST FUNCTION

From the total cost function, we can also derive the short-run marginal cost function, as

$$M = \frac{dT}{dy} = nc^{-n} y^{n-1} P_x \qquad \qquad \cdots \cdots \text{(7)}$$

Where marginal cost M being the derivative of total cost with respect to output.

CHAPTER 3

Factor–Factor Relationships

In the previous chapter our concern was about the use of a single resource and a single product, where the production function is of the nature $Y = f(X_1/X_2 X_3 X_4 ... X_n)$, where X_1 resource is variable and all other resources are held constant. But the producers use more than one resource in the production of a product. For example, in the production of rice crop the farmers use seed, different types and brands of fertilisers, pesticides, machines, human labour—both hired and owned, etc. In any production process, the producer should choose various combinations of all the factors of production within the limitations of his investment capacity. The economic level of output from a combination of fixed factors depends on the manner in which the variable resources are combined. Therefore, the important aspect of the study of factor-factor relationship is to find out the possibilities of substituting or combining two or more resources in the production of a given output level, which is economic. We study the factor–factor relationship with different combinations of two resources, keeping the output level constant at a particular level. We start the study with two resource combinations, for simplicity of understanding to the reader.

The production function can be expressed in this case as $Y = f(X_1 X_2 / X_3 X_4 ... X_n)$ or $Y = f(X_1 X_2)$, i.e. X_1 and X_2 are variable resources and other resources are held constant to produce a given level of output. The objectives of studying factor–factor relationship and substituting one resource for the other is two-fold.

1) Minimisation of cost to a given level of output of a product.
2) Optimisation of output to the fixed producing unit through alternative resource use combinations.

Optimisation of output or profit maximisation actually involves the cost minimisation in the use of variable resource. There will be large number of resource combinations, which will produce different levels of output. But only one combination will give the maximum output with least cost. The question here is of finding out optimum or least cost combination of two or more resources in producing a given amount of output.

Iso-quants

Iso-product curves show all the possible combinations of two-inputs, physically capable of producing the same amount of output or a given output level.

Iso-product curve (Fig. 3.1) represents those combinations, which will allow the production of an equal quantity of output, the producer would be indifferent between them. Therefore, these curves are called product indifference curves. They are also known as iso-quants or equal-product curves. 'Iso' meaning equal and 'quant' meaning quantity.

Input combination	X_1	X_2
A	1	12
B	2	8
C	3	5
D	4	3
E	5	2

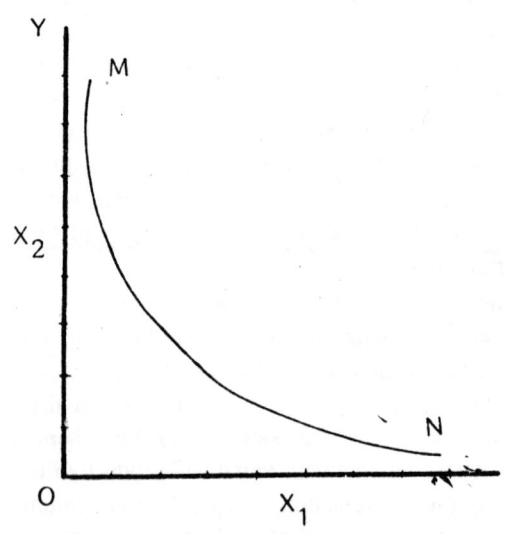

Fig. 3.1. Iso-quant.

All the input combinations of X_1 and X_2 lie on the iso-product curve and give the same output. A map (Fig. 3.2) showing different levels of output or different iso-product curves is known as iso-product contour.

Any isoline always refers to an equal quantity. Iso-product contours (iso-quant map) indicate the shape of production surface, which in turn indicates the nature of output response to the inputs.

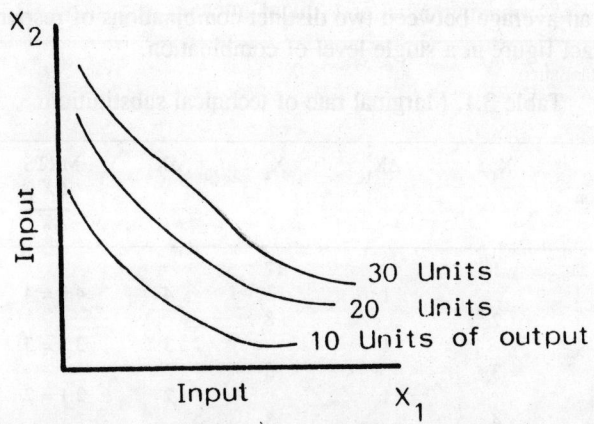

Fig. 3.2. Iso-quant map.

CHARACTERISTICS OF ISO-PRODUCT CURVES

1) *Convex to the origin*: This is due to the fact that the marginal rate of technical substitution (MRTS) fall, as more and more of X_1 is substituted for X_2.

2) They do not intersect each other, since each line refers to a different quantity of output.

3) *Sloping downwards*: From left to right (slope decreases from left to right). This is because, as the quantity of a factor X_1 is increased the quantity of factor X_2 must be decreased, so as to maintain the same level of output.

4) Higher the output, the farther away it is from the origin.

5) The slope of iso-quant denotes the rate of substitution between the two resources.

Marginal Rate of Technical Substitution (MRTS)

The marginal rate of technical substitution determines the rate, at which two resources can be substituted, i.e. how much the use of one resource can be reduced in order to add additional unit of the other factor, in such a way as to maintain the same level of output.

The rate at which one input can be replaced by one unit of the other input. The slope of the iso-product curve determines the marginal rate of substitution, as indicated in Fig. 3.3 with output remaining constant, and the slope is given by units of change in replaced resource, divided by the units of change in added resource. The MRS can be calculated in the form of an average between two distinct combinations of resources, or as an exact figure at a single level of combination.

Table 3.1. Marginal rate of technical substitution

Input combination	X_1	ΔX_1	X_2	ΔX_2	MRTS $\dfrac{\Delta X_2}{\Delta X_1}$	Output (qtl)
A	1		12			40
		1		4	4:1 = 4	40
B	2		8			40
		1		3	3:1 = 3	
C	3		5			40
		1		2	2:1 = 2	
D	4		3			40
		1		1	1:1 = 1	
E	5		2			40

$$\text{MRTS} = \frac{\Delta X_2}{\Delta X_1} = \frac{\text{No. of units of replaced resource}}{\text{No. of units of added resource}}$$

(Substitution Ratio)

The MRS of X_2 for X_1 is denoted as $\dfrac{\Delta X_1}{\Delta X_2}$.

The MRS of X_1 for X_2 is denoted as $\dfrac{\Delta X_2}{\Delta X_1}$.

In Table 3.1, we substitute X_1 for X_2, hence the MRS is $\dfrac{\Delta X_2}{\Delta X_1}$ for 40 qtl of output level. In the A combination, when we increase one unit of X_1, the amount of X_2 that need to be replaced is 4 units and the MRS ratio is 4. Likewise for every unit increase of X_1, the units of X_2 to be replaced changes from 3 units to 2 units and then to 1 unit. The rate of factor substitution is negative in all rational areas of production, and hence we do not always bother to include minus sign.

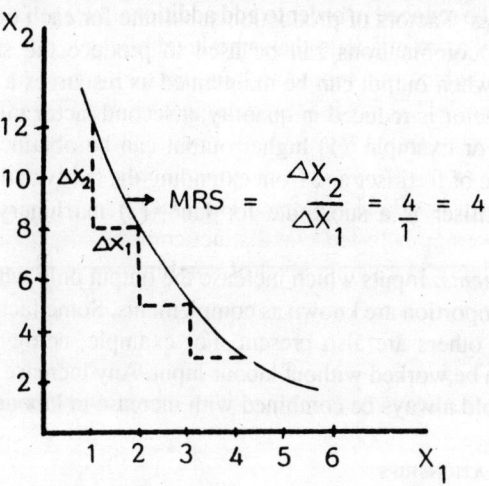

Fig. 3.3. Marginal rate of technical substitution.

ELASTICITY OF SUBSTITUTION (Es)

The elasticity of substitution is the relative change, by which factors combine in producing a constant output on a production contour and can be defined as the percentage change in one factor, divided by the percentage change in the other factor, i.e.

$$\frac{\dfrac{\Delta X_1}{X_1} \times 100}{\dfrac{\Delta X_2}{X_2} \times 100} = \frac{\dfrac{\Delta X_1}{X_1}}{\dfrac{\Delta X_2}{X_2}} = Es$$

$$\text{or } \frac{\Delta X_1}{X_1} \cdot \frac{X_2}{\Delta X_2} = \frac{\Delta X_1}{\Delta X_2} \cdot \frac{X_2}{X_1} = Es \ .$$

The elasticity is always negative for substitute resources and indicates how fast the slope of a product contour changes. *Es* can be computed either as arc elasticity or point elasticity. Arc elasticity refers to substitution over an entire portion of a product contour. Point elasticity refers to the elasticity at one particular factor combination and therefore corresponds to the exact marginal rate of substitution.

Substitutes and Complementary Resources

Substitutes: Factors of production substitute for each other, in so far as different combinations can be used to produce the same level of output, i.e. when output can be maintained as resources are reshuffled; when one factor is reduced in quantity, a second factor must always be increased. For example, (1) higher output can be obtained from more intensive use of fertiliser and from extending the cultivated areas. In this respect, fertiliser is a substitute for land, (2) machinery for bullock power.

Complements: Inputs which increase the output only when combined in a fixed proportion are known as complements. Some factors cannot be used unless others are also present. For example, neither tractors nor bullocks can be worked without labour input. Any increase in number of tractors should always be combined with increase in labour, i.e. drivers.

Perfect Relationships

At opposite extremes of the factor–factor relationship are perfect substitutes and perfect complements. Perfectly substitutable factors replace each other at a constant rate, regardless of the level of output, or of the proportion in which the factors are combined. For example, family and hired labour, different brands of same fertiliser, home grown grain and purchased grain. With perfect substitutes, iso-product curve in Fig. 3.4 is a straight line, intersecting the axes. Output can be increased by using a little more of one factor alone, or more of both factors together.

Perfect Complements

Show contrasting characteristics to perfect substitutes, in that no production results, if either factors is used separately. Factors can be combined only in certain fixed proportions. The iso-product curve (Fig. 3.5) in this case is of a right angle. For example, tractor hours and 8 man hours.

Imperfect Relationships

Although perfect factor relationships are not by themselves of great direct significance in agriculture, the more common shape of iso-product curves for agricultural factors is the convexity towards the origin (Fig. 3.6).

Over the middle portion of such curves factors are good substitutes, but tend to approach a complementary relationship at either extreme.

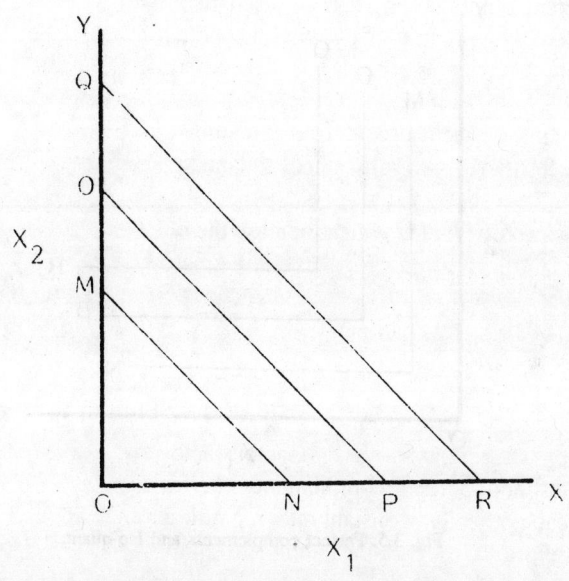

Fig 3.4. Perfect substitutes and the Iso-quant.

Types of Resource—Combination
(Types of factor—factor combination)

The shapes of the iso-quants and production surface will depend upon the manner in which the variable inputs are combined to produce a particular level of output. There can be three categories of such combinations of inputs.

1) Fixed pi portion combination of inputs
2) Constant rate of substitution
3) Varying rates of substitution

1) FIXED PROPORTION COMBINATION OF INPUTS

There are certain enterprises or products which can only be produced if inputs are added in fixed proportion at all levels of production. In these cases there is no decision problem, because the inputs combine in a fixed proportion. There is only one way of combining inputs which will produce given level of product, represented by the product contour. Iso-

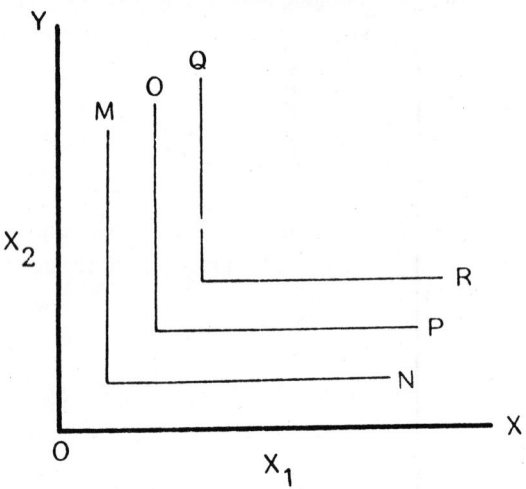

Fig. 3.5. Perfect complements and Iso-quant.

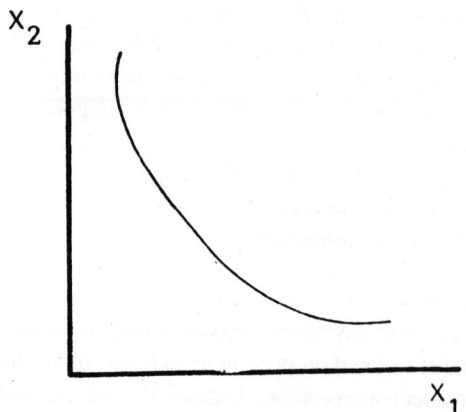

Fig. 3.6. Imperfect relationship.

quants are 'L' (right angle) shaped and factors are perfect complements. The examples of fixed proportion combinations of resources are more common in the combination of chemical compounds, i.e. for the formation of H_2O (water molecule), we require one atom of oxygen and two atoms of hydrogen. The increase in one element alone cannot increase the output, unless the other element is combined in fixed proportions.

In Fig. 3.7, to produce 50 units of a product we require an input level OA of resource X_2 and OC of resource X_1. If input X_2 is increased to OB, while X_2 is held at OC the output remains at 50. An increase in X_1 to OD while X_2 is constant does not add to the total product. However, a simultaneous increase in X_1 to OD and X_2 to OB results in a doubling of the product, as the factors are held in fixed proportions. Here we consider both the factors X_1 and X_2 to be limitational factors, since output is limited by input of either. A factor which is limitational in the sense as above, has a marginal productivity zero when this alone is increased in quantity.

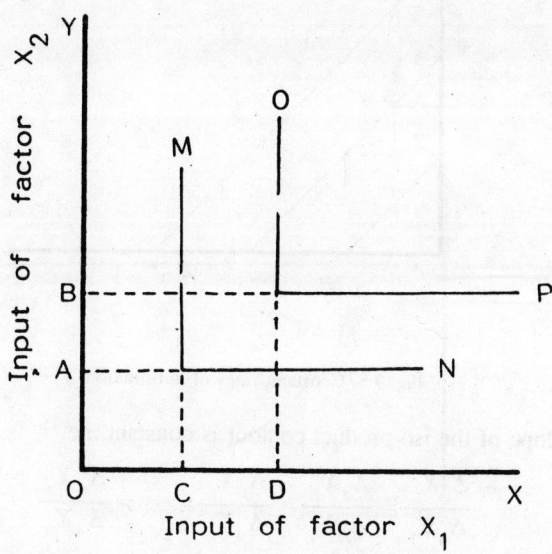

Fig. 3.7. Fixed proportion combination of Inputs.

2) CONSTANT RATE OF SUBSTITUTION

The substitution at constant rate takes place, when the rate of replacement of one resource by the other resource does not change as the added input increases in magnitude. Linear iso-product lines (Fig 3.8) characterise resources which substitute at constant rate (straight lines). One unit of X_1 substitutes for two units of X_2, conversely one unit of X_2 substitute for 0.5 units of X_1. The substitution ratio is constant through all combinations of the two factors. The change in X_1 is 5 and change in X_2 is 10 between any two levels of combinations. The MRS of X_1 for X_2, i.e.

$$\frac{\Delta X_2}{\Delta X_1} = \frac{10}{5} = 2; \text{ conversely the MRS of } X_2 \text{ for } X_1 \text{ } \frac{\Delta X_1}{\Delta X_2} = \frac{5}{10} = 0.5.$$

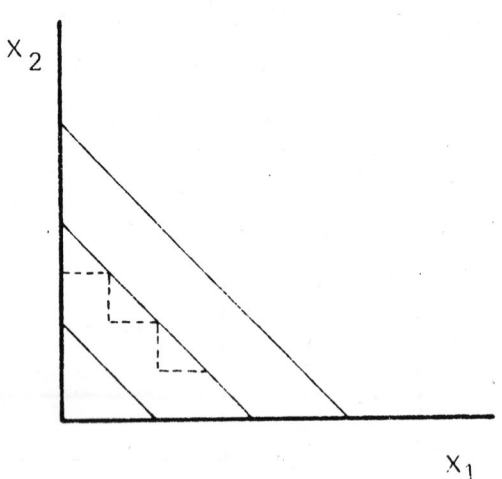

Fig. 3.8. Constant rates of substitution.

The slope of the iso-product contour is constant, i.e.

$$\frac{\Delta_1 X_2}{\Delta_1 X_1} = \frac{\Delta_2 X_2}{\Delta_2 X_1} = \frac{\Delta_3 X_2}{\Delta_3 X_1} = \cdots = \frac{\Delta_n X_2}{\Delta_n X_1}$$

When the inputs substitute at constant rate, only one will be used, which one to use depends upon relative prices.

3) VARYING RATES OF SUBSTITUTION

The amount of one input (X_1) required to substitute for one unit of another input (X_2) at a given level of production increases or decreases as the amount of X_1 used increases. Hence there can be either increasing rate of substitution, or decreasing rate of substitution.

Substitution at an increasing rate is not commonly available. Substitution at decreasing rate is the more common case in agriculture. In this case, the slope of iso-product curve (Fig. 3.9) becomes less steep as more of X_1 is used relative to X_2. The MRS of X_1 becomes smaller and smaller as X_1 continuously replaces X_2 with constant output. Increasingly greater quantities of X_1 are required to off-set or replace each successive decrease in X_2 resource. Each unit of added X_1 substitutes less of X_2 than the previous one.

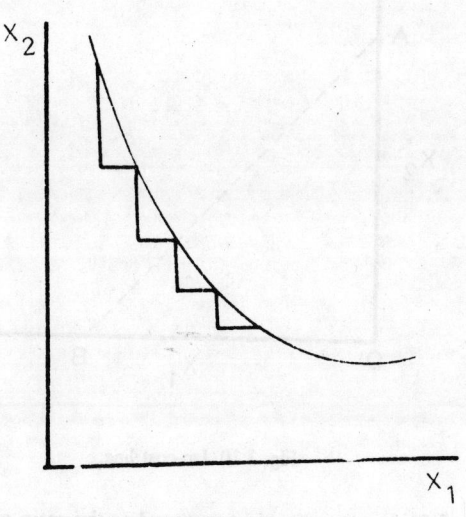

Fig. 3.9. Decreasing rates of substitution.

Substitution ratio changes as under:

$$\frac{\Delta_1 X_2}{\Delta_1 X_1} > \frac{\Delta_2 X_2}{\Delta_2 X_1} > \cdots > \frac{\Delta_n X_2}{\Delta_n X_1}$$

Thus every subsequent increase in the use of one factor replaces less and less of the other in decreasing rates of substitution.

Iso-cost lines (Equal cost lines, price line or outlay line)

Iso-cost lines indicate all possible combinations of two inputs, which can be purchased at a given cost with a given outlay of investment fund.

Suppose a farmer has Rs. 100 to spend on two resources X_1 and X_2, when price of X_1 is Rs. 5 and that of X_2 is Rs. 10 per unit. Then he can purchase either 20 units of X_1 or 10 units of X_2. When these two points are connected on a diagram by a line, we get the iso-cost line (Fig. 3.10).

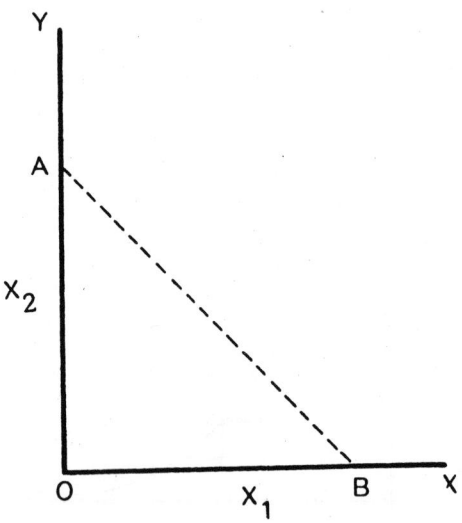

Fig. 3.10. Iso-cost line.

The slope of the iso-cost line is expressed as the ratio of the price of one input to the price of another input. Thus the slope of iso-cost line is PX_1/PX_2 and they are linear and determined by end points. AB is an iso-cost line. Assuming that the price of a unit of X_1 is PX_1 and that of X_2 is PX_2, the number of units which can be purchased with M units of money is:

$$\frac{M}{PX_1} \text{ and } \frac{M}{PX_2}$$ respectively. The slope of iso-cost line is: AO/OB, i.e

$$\frac{M}{PX_2} \bigg/ \frac{M}{PX_1} = \frac{\text{Units of } X_2}{\text{Units of } X_1}$$

$$\frac{\dfrac{M}{PX_2}}{\dfrac{M}{PX_1}} = \frac{M}{PX_2} \cdot \frac{PX_1}{M} = \frac{PX_1}{PX_2}$$

PROPERTIES OF ISO-COST LINE

1) *Distance of iso-cost line from the origin*: Under constant price situation, each possible total outlay has a different iso-cost line. As outlay increases, the iso-cost line moves higher and higher, farther away from the origin (Fig. 3.11).

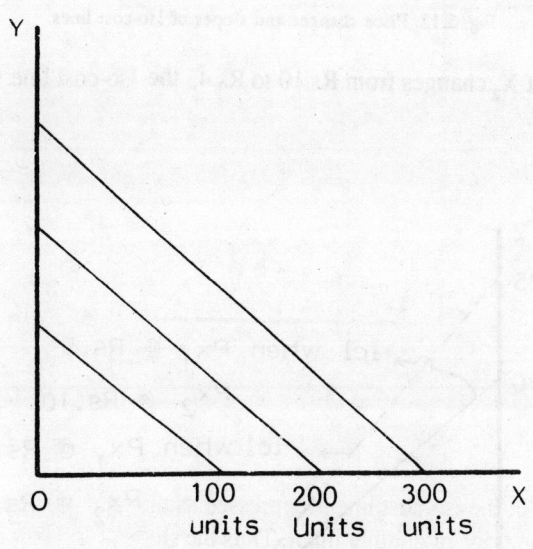

Fig 3.11. Distance of Iso-cost line and total outlay.

2) The slope of the iso-cost line indicates the ratio of factor prices. Changes in the input-price ratio will change the slope of the iso-cost line.

1. If price of X_1 changes from Rs 5 to Rs 10, the Iso-cost line will be as in Fig. 3.12.

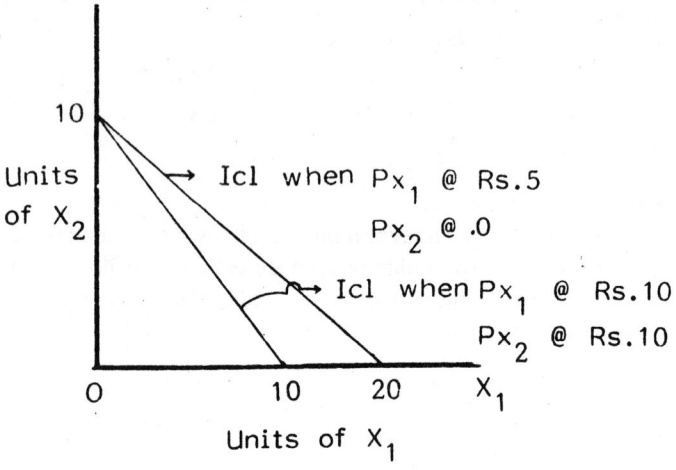

Fig. 3.12. Price changes and slopes of Iso-cost lines.

2. If price of X_2 changes from Rs 10 to Rs 4, the Iso-cost line will be as in Fig. 3.13.

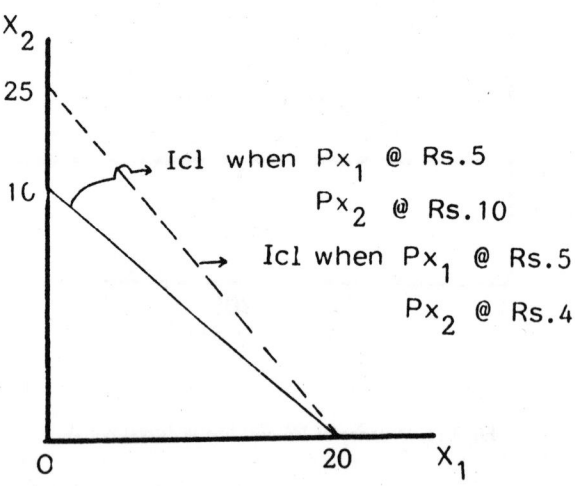

Fig. 3.13. Price changes and slopes of Iso-cost lines.

(a) the price of X_1 changes from Rs. 5 to 10 and (b) price of X_2 from Rs. 10 to 4, the iso-cost lines will be as in Fig. 3.12.

Principle of cost minimisation

Rational resource combinations have been defined as those falling on the portion of the iso-quant contour with negative marginal rates of substitution between factors, i.e. an increase in one factor allows a decrease in another. Since an input-output relationship or production function gives rise to both factor–product and factor–factor relationships, the two questions of (i) the optimum yield or output level and (ii) the optimum combination of variable resources for a fixed unit, must also be decided. The problem is one of how resources should be combined for the fixed technical unit, if output is to be expanded from zero to the most profitable level (factor–product) with variable resources combined in a least cost manner (factor–factor) for each level of output. The selection of resource combination within the rational range is possible only by means of a choice indicator. The relevant choice indicator for profit maximisation is the factor–price ratio.

The principle of cost minimisation (least cost combination of resources) can be defined as "if two or more factors are employed in production of a single product, cost is at a minimum when the ratio of factor prices is inversely equal to the marginal rate of substitution of factors".

Algebraic expression of cost minimisation

i) Compute the marginal rate of substituion ratio

$$\text{i.e. } \frac{\Delta X_2}{\Delta X_1} = \frac{\text{No. of units of replaced resource}}{\text{No. of units of added resource}}.$$

ii) Compute price ratio $= \dfrac{PX_1}{PX_2} = \dfrac{\text{Cost per unit of added resource}}{\text{Cost per unit of replaced resource}}$

iii) Workout the least cost combination by equating:

$$\frac{\Delta X_2}{\Delta X_1} = \frac{PX_1}{PX_2} \text{ for MRS of } X_1 \text{ for } X_2.$$

Cost of adding X_1 is equal to the reduction in cost from X_2.

$$\frac{PX_1}{PX_2} < \frac{\Delta X_2}{\Delta X_1} = \text{Cost can be lessened by using more of } X_1 \text{ and less of } X_2.$$

$$\frac{PX_2}{PX_1} < \frac{\Delta X_1}{\Delta X_2} = \quad \text{Cost can be lessened by using more of } X_2 \text{ and less of } X_1.$$

This can be written as: $PX_2 \cdot \Delta X_2 = PX_1 \cdot \Delta X_1$.

If at any point on the iso-quant, $PX_2 \cdot \Delta X_2$ is greater than $P X_1 \cdot \Delta X_1$, then the cost of producing the given output could be produced by increasing the use of X_1 and decreasing X_2, because the cost of added unit of X_1 is less than the cost of the replaced units of X_2. On the other hand, if at any point on the iso-quant $PX_2 \cdot \Delta X_2$ is less than $PX_1 \cdot \Delta X_1$, the cost of producing the specified amount of output can be reduced by using less of X_1 and more of X_2.

This equality criterion signifies that any change in the input combination from this point would increase cost of producing the output.

GRAPHIC METHOD

Since the slope of iso-cost line indicates the ratio of factor prices and the slope of iso-product curve represents the marginal rate of substitution, the point of factor combination at minimum cost for a given output is at the point of tangency of these iso-lines. (Fig 3.14.)

$\therefore$ Slope of iso-quant $=$ Slope of iso-cost line

$$\text{i.e. } \frac{\Delta X_2}{\Delta X_1} = \frac{PX_1}{PX_2}$$

This equality defines the condition which applies at the point of least cost combination of inputs. The above equation can be expressed in other terms. Any movement down the iso-product curve results from partial withdrawal of X_2 and a compensating increase in X_1 (to maintain Y constant). The change in the output, in absolute terms, resulting from compensating the addition of X_1. Therefore

$$\Delta X_2 \cdot MPP_{X_2} = \Delta X_1 \cdot MPP_{X_1}, \text{ i.e. } \frac{\Delta X_2}{\Delta X_1} = \frac{MPP_{X_1}}{MPP_{X_2}}.$$

It has been shown that the point of least-cost combination (LCC) is given by:

$$\frac{\Delta X_2}{\Delta X_1} = \frac{PX_1}{PX_2}.$$

$$\therefore \frac{MPP_{X_1}}{MPP_{X_2}} = \frac{PX_1}{PX_2}$$

$$\text{or } MPP_{X_2} \quad PX_1 = MPP_{X_1} \cdot PX_2.$$

$$\therefore \frac{MPP_{X_1}}{P_{X_1}} = \frac{MPP_{X_2}}{P_{X_2}}.$$

In other words, economic combination of factors is achieved when the return from the marginal rupee spent on one factor is equal to return from the marginal rupee spent on the other factor.

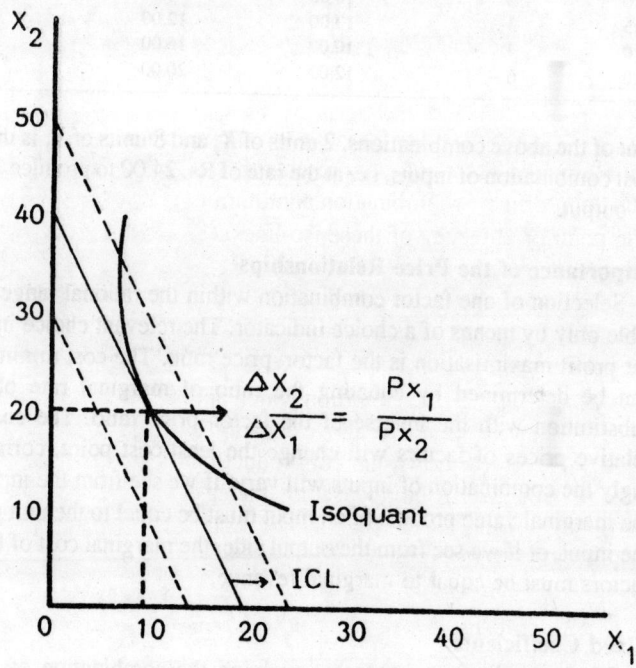

Fig. 3.14. Least cost combination of factors.

ARITHMETICAL CALCULATION OF LEAST COST

One possible way to determine the least-cost combination is to compute the cost of all possible combinations and then select the one with minimum cost. Suppose there are five combinations of inputs which can produce 25 units of output. The price per unit of X_1 is Rs. 2 and of X_2 is Rs. 4. The outlay of each combination can be determined as follows (Table 3.2):

Table 3.2. Estimation of least cost by simple arithmetics

X_1	X_2	Cost of X_1 @ Rs.2	Cost of X_2 @ Rs 4	Total outlay of X_1 & X_2 (Rs.) to produce 25 units of output
12.0	1	24.00	4.00	28.00
8.0	2	16.00	8.00	24.00
6.5	3	13.00	12.00	25.00
5.0	4	10.00	16.00	26.00
3.0	6	12.00	20.00	32.00

Out of the above combinations, 2 units of X_2 and 8 units of X_1 is the least-cost combination of inputs, i.e: at the rate of Rs. 24.00 to produce 25 units of output.

Importance of the Price Relationships

Selection of one factor combination within the rational range is possible only by means of a choice indicator. The relevant choice indicator for profit maximisation is the factor-price ratio. The cost minimisation can be determined by equating the ratio of marginal rate of factor substitution with the inverse of the factor-price ratio. The change in relative prices of factors will change the least-cost point, correspondingly the combination of inputs will vary. If we see from the input side, the marginal value product of an input must be equal to the unit price of the input, or if we see from the output side, the marginal cost of both the factors must be equal to marginal revenue.

Fixed Coefficients

Of the production processes involving the combination of two resources in fixed proportions, only one resource combination is possible, because the factors must be combined in the manner dictated by this extreme technique of production. Either it does or does not pay to combine resources in the fixed proportions and produce the product. The only economic question is, is the marginal value of the product greater than the marginal cost of the two factors combined?

CONSTANT RATES OF SUBSTITUTION

If two factors (X_1 and X_2) substitute at constant marginal rates, only one of the two unique combinations will give the least-cost combinations to produce a given output. The given output should be produced exclusively with X_1 and none of X_2, or entirely with X_2 and none of X_1. In Table 3.3, X_1 and X_2 resources substitute each other at a constant rate of 4.0 or 0.25. When the price of X_1 is Rs.4 and the price of X_2 is Rs. 2, the cost of producing 100 units of product is minimum when 50 units of X_1 and none of X_2 (situation 1), or when the price of X_1 is Rs. 10 and X_2 is Rs.2, the same amount of output can be produced with X_2 alone (situation 2). In the third situation, any one of the given factor combinations can be used, which results in the same cost outlay, and the substitution is equal to the price ratio for all the combinations. In situation 1, the substitution ratio is greater than the price ratio; then X_1 should always be used by replacing X_2 as 10 units of X_1 with a total cost of Rs. 40, replaces 40 units of X_2 with total cost of Rs. 80. In situation 2, X_2 resources should be used (Rs. 80 total cost) at the expense of X_1 resource costing Rs. 100, because the substitution ratio is less than price ratio.

Table 3.3. Constant rates of substitution

X_1	X_2	$\dfrac{\Delta X_2}{\Delta X_1}$	$\dfrac{\Delta X_1}{\Delta X_2}$	Cost of 100 units of Y with factor prices per unit of		
				X_1 @ Rs.4 X_2 @ Rs.2	X_1 @ Rs.10 X_2 @ Rs.2	X_1 @ Rs.16 X_2 @ Rs.4
0	200			400	400	800
10	160	$\dfrac{-40}{10} = -4$	$\dfrac{10}{40} = -0.25$	360	420	800
20	120	$\dfrac{-40}{10} = -4$	$\dfrac{10}{40} = -0.25$	320	440	800
30	80	$\dfrac{-40}{10} = -4$	$\dfrac{10}{40} = -0.25$	280	460	800
40	40	$\dfrac{-40}{10} = -4$	$\dfrac{10}{40} = -0.25$	240	480	800
50	0	$\dfrac{-40}{10} = -4$	$\dfrac{10}{40} = -0.25$	200	500	800

Situation 1: Price ratio = 2; Situation 2: Price ratio = 5; Situation 3: Price ratio = 4.0.

DECREASING RATES OF SUBSTITUTION

In Table 3.4 when X_1 and X_2 resources are priced at Rs. 1.60 and

Re. 1.00 respectively, they substitute at a decreasing rate and the minimum cost of combining these two resources is at Rs. 83 when the price ratio is 1.60, which is equal to the substitution ratio in the range 1.70–1.10. Similarly, when the price ratio is 1.05, the minimum cost of combining X_1 and X_2 is in the range 1.10–0.90 of substitution ratio's, i.e. the inputs should be combined between 40 and 50 units of X_1 and 24 and 15 units of X_2.

Table 3.4. Decreasing rates of substitution

X_1	X_2	$\dfrac{\Delta X_2}{\Delta X_1}$	Cost of 100 units of Y with factor prices	
			at X_1 @ Rs. 1.60 X_2 @ Re. 1.00	X_1 @ Rs. 2.10 X_2 @ Rs. 2.00
10	70		86.00	161.00
20	52	−1.80	84.08	146.00
30	35	−1.70	83.00	133.00
40	24	−1.10	88.00	132.00
50	15	−0.90	95.00	135.00

$$\frac{P\,X_1}{P\,X_2} = 1.60; \qquad \frac{P\,X_1}{P\,X_2} = 1.05.$$

Isoclines, Ridge lines and Expansion path

A line or curve connecting the least cost combination of inputs for all output levels is known as isocline. Isoclines connect the points of equal slope or equal MRS on successively higher iso-quants.

This line shows that the resources should be used as long as the MVP is greater than MC of the resources used. They can be drawn at different sets of price ratios (Fig. 3.15).

All isoclines converge at the point of maximum output if the maximum exists.

RIDGE LINES

Ridge lines are the border lines which separate complementarity from substitution. They are called special types of isoclines, joining points of equal slopes via iso-product curves. These lines denote the limits of economic relevance, as the boundaries beyond which isocline and iso-quant maps cease to have any economic meaning. Ridge lines represent the points of maximum output from each input, given a fixed amount of other input. In the areas outside the ridge line, factors are complements, since both the factors are required in larger quantities to increase output. Both the factors serve in complementary capacity for the family of contours indicated in Fig. 3.16.

If output is to be held at 10, X_2 can be substituted for X_1 only until contour line $I_1 P_1$ becomes vertical. Conversely X_1 can be substituted for X_2 only up to the point where $I_1 P_1$ becomes horizontal. The two resources are substituted inside the ranges traced out by the border or ridge lines *OA* and *OB*.

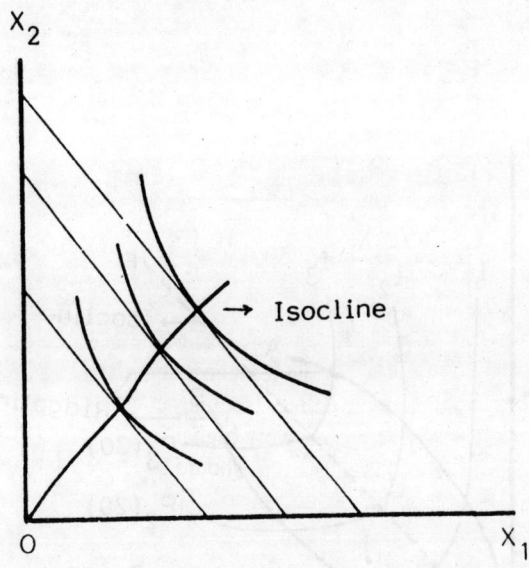

Fig. 3.15. Isoclines.

The resources X_1 and X_2 are complements for combinations falling outside of the border lines. For the vertical portions of the product contours above *OA*, X_1 is complementary with X_2: (a) no increase in product is forthcoming unless X_1 is increased along with X_2, while (b) no amount of X_2 will substitute for X_1, if the product is not to be decreased.

For the horizontal portions of the contours below *OB*, the same conditions hold in respect to the relationship of X_2 with X_1. In the case of fixed coefficients, the two strictly limitational factors are technical complements throughout and the borderlines merge, until they coincide at OF. In the case of resources which substitute at constant rates throughout all possible combinations, the border lines diverse until they become identical with X and Y axes. In Fig. 3.16, MRS of X_1 for X_2, i.e. $\dfrac{\Delta X_2}{\Delta X_1}$ is zero at 10 output and X_2 is at minimum of OT. If X_1 is increased beyond OR, none of X_2 is replaced. Between X_1 inputs of OR and OS, the ratio is O/RS or zero. Between the ridge lines the MRS is less than zero, i.e. $\dfrac{\Delta X_2}{\Delta X_1}$ or $\dfrac{\Delta X_1}{\Delta X_2}$ must be negative, since a positive change in one factor must always be associated with a negative change in the other.

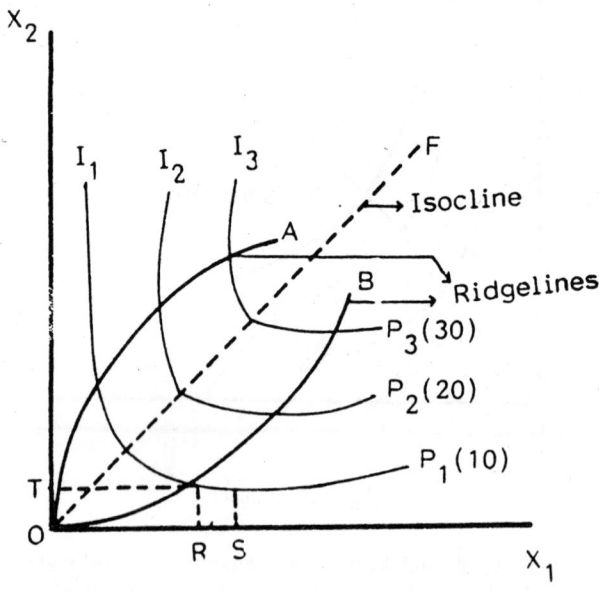

Fig. 3.16. Ridge lines.

EXPANSION PATH

Each level of output or iso-product curve will have its own particular least-cost combination of factors. There can be numerous isoclines for different possible combinations of input prices. All these sets of prices of inputs do not prevail at any particular given time. A farm manager has to consider only one set of input prices, which he may think to be the most appropriate for the planning periods to a given level of output. The isocline dependent upon this set of prices is called expansion path.

If all the least-cost combination points are joined to each other, the result is an expansion line. Since with factor–price ratio constant for each level of output, the MRS between factors is the same for each level of output (tangency of isoclines), thus the expansion line is an isocline. Of the many isoclines, the isocline which is considered to be most appropriate over a production period is known as expansion path (Fig. 3.17). At any particular time only one expansion path is possible.

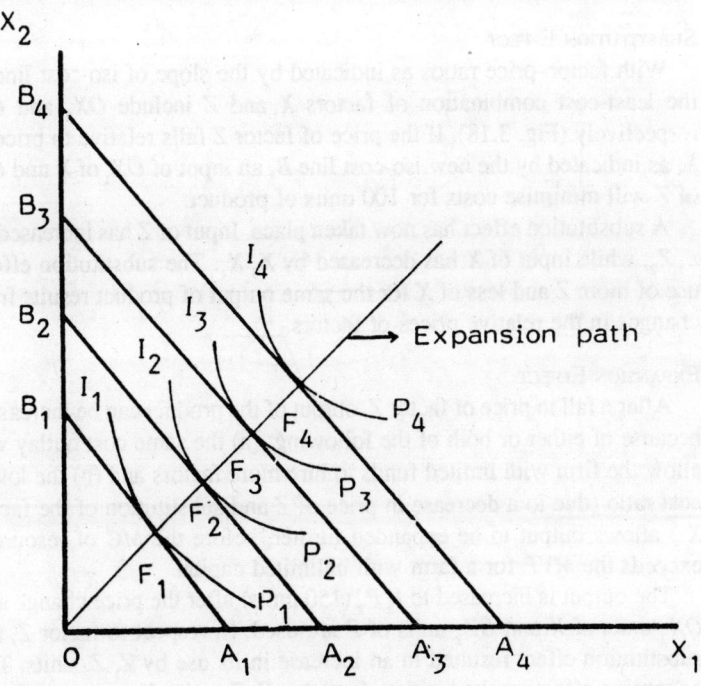

Fig. 3.17. Expansion path.

$I_1 P_1, I_2 P_2, I_3 P_3$ and $I_4 P_4$ are iso-product contours. Given the prices of inputs A_1 B_1, A_2 B_2, A_3 B_3 and A_4 B_4 are iso-cost lines with different expenditure limits. F_1, F_2, F_3, F_4 are different tangency points of iso-cost line with iso-quants. The expansion line is drawn through minimum-cost lines and indicates how the relative proportions of the factors changes as output is increased and if costs are minimised for each particular output. Output should be expanded along expansion line, as long as the marginal value product is greater than the marginal cost of the resources added. The MPP is the difference in output represented by the series of contours, while the added resources are indicated on the X and Y axes.

Substitution Effects and Expansion Effects

Changes in the price of factors can give rise to two types of adjustments: (1) substitution effect and (2) expansion effect. These adjustments apply equally to farm-firm, which have limited and unlimited capital and can produce only the quantity attainable with given resources.

SUBSTITUTION EFFECT

With factor–price ratios as indicated by the slope of iso-cost line A, the least-cost combination of factors X and Z include OX_3 and OZ_1 respectively (Fig. 3.18). If the price of factor Z falls relative to price of X, as indicated by the new iso-cost line B, an input of OX_1 of X and OZ_2 of Z will minimise costs for 100 units of product.

A substitution effect has now taken place. Input of Z has increased by $Z_1 Z_2$, while input of X has decreased by $X_3 X_1$. The substitution effect, use of more Z and less of X for the same output of product results from changes in the relative prices of factors.

EXPANSION EFFECT

After a fall in price of factor Z, output of the product can be increased, because of either or both of the following: (a) the same cost outlay will allow the firm with limited funds to hire more factors and (b) the lower cost ratio (due to a decrease in price of Z and substitution of the factor X) allows output to be expanded further, before the MC of resources exceeds the MVP for a farm with unlimited capital.

The output is increased to $I_2 P_2$ (150 units) after the price change and OX_2 units of X and OZ_3 units of Z are used. In respect to factor Z, the substitution effect resulted in an increase in its use by $Z_1 Z_2$ units. The expansion effect resulted in use of another $Z_2 Z_3$ units. In respect to factor X, the expansion effect partially offsets the substitution effect, while the substitution effect reduced the use of X by $X_1 X_3$ units, the expansion effect restores $X_1 X_2$ units to use.

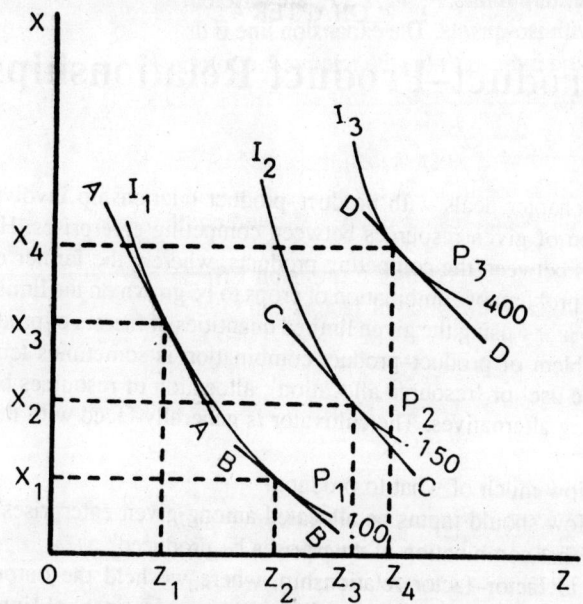

Fig. 3.18. Substitution effects and expansion effects.

Economic Complements

It is also possible for the expansion effect to result in increased use of both the factors. In Fig. 3.18. the expansion effect is so great that it carries output to $I_3 P_3$ (400 units), use of X will increase to OX_4, while input of Z will increase to OZ_4. This combination includes more of both factors than the original quantities of OX_3 and OZ_1. Factor X and Z have now become economic complements.

When two factors X and Z can be used in producing a single commodity Y, and a fall in the price of factor Z leads to an increase in output of Y and an increase in use of both the factors X and Z, the factors are economic complements.

If more of factor Z is used while less of factor X is used, with output of Y increasing or remaining the same, the two factors are economic substitutes or rivals. Technical complementarity always leads to economic complementarity. However, two factors can be economic complements, eventhough they are technical substitutes.

CHAPTER 4

Product–Product Relationships

This chapter deals with product–product relationship involving the allocation of given resources between competing enterprises. Here the choice is between the competing products, wherein the farmer is faced with the problem of combination of crops to be grown on the limited area of the farm, by using the given limited quantities of factors of production. The problem of product–product combination is sometimes termed as 'resource use' or 'resource allocation'; allocation of resources between competing alternatives. The cultivator is generally faced with the question of:

1) How much of what to produce?
2) How should inputs be allocated among given enterprises?
3) What combination of enterprises be produced?

Similar to factor–factor relationship, where we held the output level constant and choose between different combinations of inputs for realising a certain level of output, in product–product relationship we held factor use constant and choose between various combinations of products. The objectives of product–product relationships are:

1) Profit maximisation with a given resource allocation, when two or more products are being produced.

2) To determine the best combination of products for a given outlay of resources.

Algebraically this relationship can be written as $Y_1 = f(Y_2)$; when more than two products are involved $Y_1 = f(Y_2, Y_3, Y_4,....,Y_n)$. When resources are fixed in quantity, the output of one of a pair of competing commodities is a function of the output of the other commodity. The production function for each of the two products takes the general form of $Y_1 = f(X_1, X_2, X_3,..., X_n)$ and $Y_2 = f(X_1, X_2, X_3, ..., X_n)$. Since the quantity of resources is constant, while products are variable, the function can be written as:

$Y_1 = f(X_1, X_2, X_3,..., X_n, Y_2)$ or simply $Y_1 = f(Y_2)$ and

$Y_2 = f(X_1, X_2, X_3,..., X_n, Y_1)$ or simply $Y_2 = f(Y_1)$.

The general equilibrium condition for a given level of inputs requires the knowledge of two relationships:

(a) production possibility curve and (b) iso-revenue line.

PRODUCTION POSSIBILITY CURVE

The production possibility curve represents all the possible combinations of two products that can be produced with given amounts of inputs.

The production possibility curves are also known as transformation curves, iso-resource curves, iso-factor curves, iso-cost curves, or iso-outlay curves. The term 'iso' means equal; equal resource curve or line indicate the possible combinations of two products, when an equal quantity of resources is available for the two products. These iso-lines are also called opportunity curves, since they indicate the opportunities or possibilities in the production of two enterprises when resources are constant.

The terms iso-cost curves or iso-outlay curves refer to a given quantity in the form of money or value.

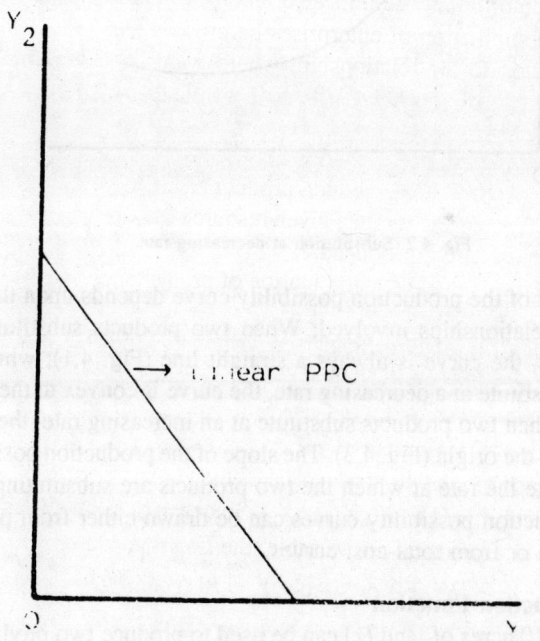

ig. 4.1. Substitution at constant rate

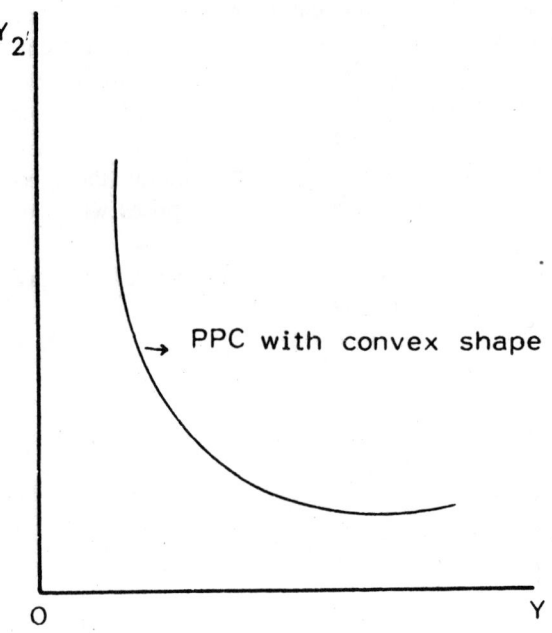

Fig. 4.2. Substitution at decreasing rate.

The shape of the production possibility curve depends upon the type of product relationships involved. When two products substitute at a constant rate, the curve is always a straight line (Fig. 4.1); when two products substitute at a decreasing rate, the curve is convex to the origin (Fig. 4.2); when two products substitute at an increasing rate, the curve is concave to the origin (Fig. 4.3). The slope of the production possibility curve indicate the rate at which the two products are substituting.

The production possibility curves can be drawn either from production function or from total-cost curves.

From Production Function

Suppose 10 acres of land (x) can be used to produce two products Y_1 and Y_2 assuming all other inputs used to produce Y_2, or Y_1 are highly specialised and fixed. The farm entrepreneur has to decide, howmuch of input (x) to use on each product. The amount of land (x) that can be used to produce Y_1 depends upon the amount of land used in producing Y_2, i.e. $Y_1 = f(Y_2)$.

Suppose production functions for two products using the same input are as under (Table 4.1):

Table 4.1. Input–output relationship for Y_1 and Y_2 products

Input (x) (acre)	Product (Y_1) Qtl.	Product (Y_2) Qtl.
1	10	8
2	17	16
3	23	24
4	28	32
5	32	40
6	35	48
7	37	56
8	38	64
9	38.50	72
10	38.80	80

The input X can be used to produce either Y_2 or Y_1 or a combination of them, as in Fig. 4.4 and Fig. 4.5.

We can determine various combinations of the two products in such a manner that a maximum of one is obtained for any level of the other. Such combinations are presented in Table 4.2.

Table 4.2. Possible product combinations from 10 acres of land

Production possibilities for 10 acres		Physical output of	
Y_2	Y_1	Y_1	Y_2
10	0	0	80
9	1	10	72
8	2	17	64
7	3	23	56
6	4	28	48
5	5	32	40
4	6	35	32
3	7	37	24
2	8	38	16
1	9	38.50	8
0	10	38.80	0

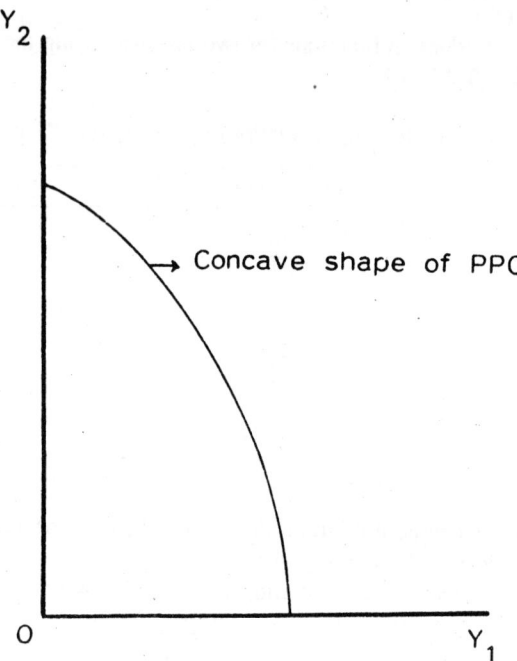

Fig. 4.3. Substitution at increasing rate.

Plotting these two functions on a graph will give the following production possibility curve (Fig. 4.6) with 10 units of input.

A production possibility curve for greater units of input will represent a higher level of production of both products and will be located farther from the origin. A production possibility curve for lesser units of input would be located closer to the origin and at lower level of production.

Marginal Rate of Production Substitution

Marginal rate of product substitution (MRPs) means the rate of change in quantity of one product as a result of an unit increase in the other product, given that the amount of the input used remains constant.

The MRPS of Y_1 for Y_2 will be $\dfrac{\Delta Y_2}{\Delta Y_1}$

and Y_2 for Y_1 will be $\dfrac{\Delta Y_1}{\Delta Y_2}$.

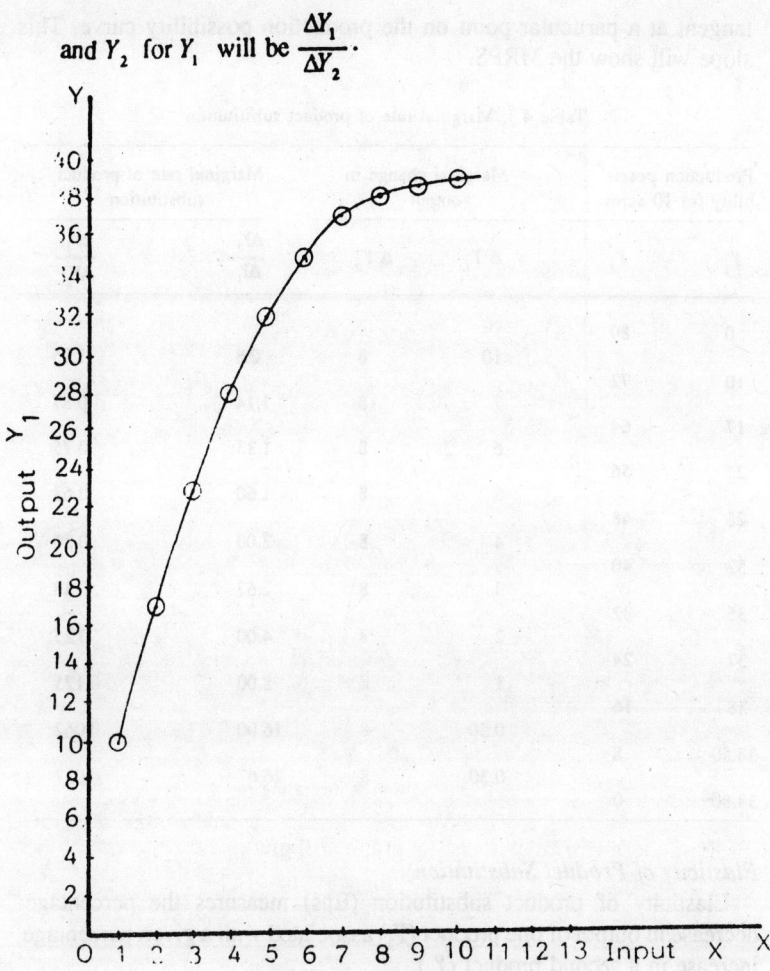

Fig. 4.4. Input-output relationship (Y_1 product).

Computations are similar to marginal rates of input substitution and marginal rates of product substitution presented in Table 4.3.

This indicates the number of units of Y_1 sacrificed for each unit of Y_2 gained, as resources are shifted to Y_2 and vice versa.

As the amount of Y_1 increases, the amount of Y_2 sacrificed increases. This is due to the decreasing marginal returns displaced by the production function. The slope of the PPC can be found out by drawing a tangent at a particular point on the production possibility curve. This slope will show the MRPS.

Table 4.3. Marginal rate of product substitution

Production possibility for 10 acres		Marginal change in output		Marginal rate of product substitution	
Y_1	Y_2	ΔY_1	ΔY_2	$\dfrac{\Delta Y_2}{\Delta Y_1}$	$\dfrac{\Delta Y_1}{\Delta Y_2}$
0	80				
		10	8	0.8	1.25
10	72				
		7	8	1.14	0.87
17	64				
		6	8	1.33	0.75
23	56				
		5	8	1.60	0.63
28	48				
		4	8	2.00	0.50
32	40				
		3	8	2.67	0.38
35	32				
		2	8	4.00	0.25
37	24				
		1	8	8.00	0.125
38	16				
		0.50	8	16.00	0.062
38.50	8				
		0.30	8	26.67	0.037
38.80	0				

Elasticity of Product Substitution

Elasticity of product substitution (Eps) measures the percentage decrease in output of one product (Y_2) associated with a given percentage increase in a second product (Y_1).

$$\text{Eps} = \frac{\dfrac{\Delta Y_2}{Y_2}}{\dfrac{\Delta Y_1}{Y_1}} \quad \text{or} \quad \frac{\Delta Y_2}{\Delta Y_1} \cdot \frac{Y_1}{Y_2}$$

As the Eps of Y_1 for Y_2 increases, the opportunity line has a greater curvature towards the axis, or an opportunity line with a high elasticity will have a much sharper curvature than the one with low elasticity.

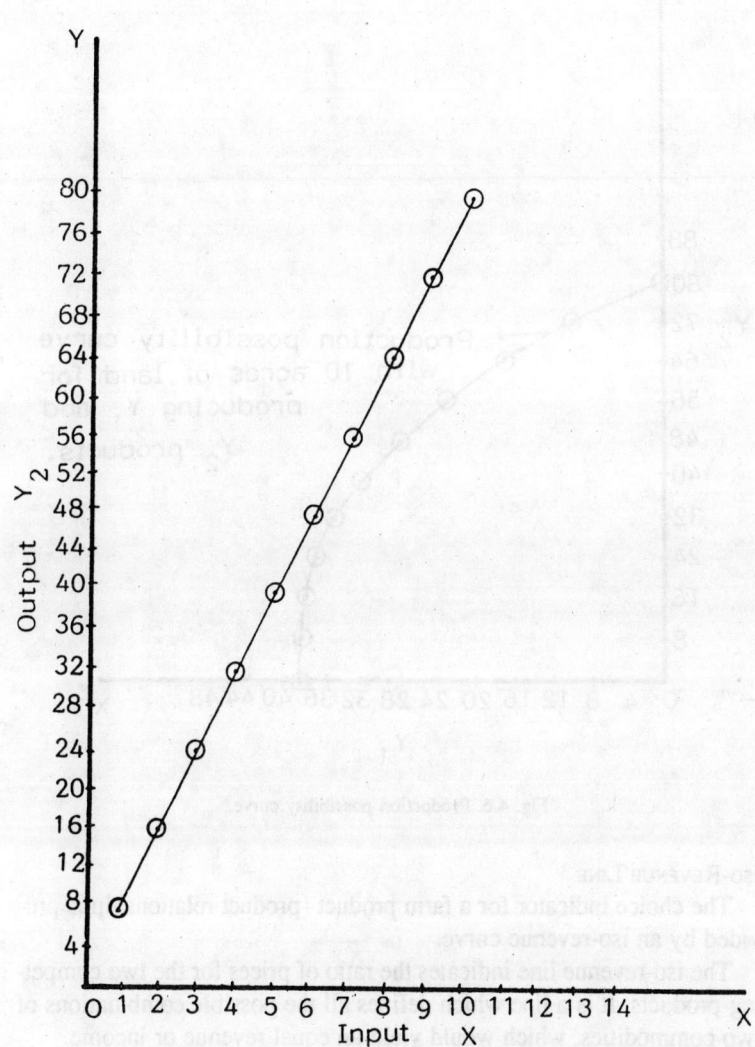

Fig. 4.5. Input–output relationship (Y_2 product).

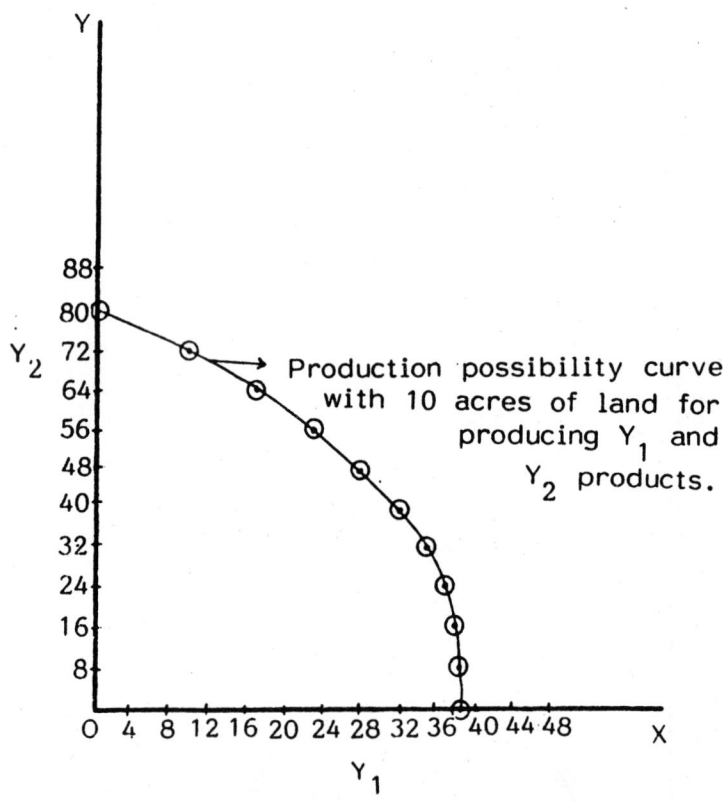

Fig. 4.6. Production possibility curve.

Iso-Revenue Line

The choice indicator for a farm product–product relationship is provided by an iso-revenue curve.

The iso-revenue line indicates the ratio of prices for the two competing products. It is a line which defines all the possible combinations of two commodities, which would yield an equal revenue or income.

In Fig. 4.7 the line *AB* is an iso-revenue line. The slope of the line is *OA/OB*. *OA* the number of units of product Y_2, *OB* the number units of Y_1 which on being sold, earn *R* units of revenue. Assuming that the relative prices are PY_1 and PY_2, the quantity $OA = \dfrac{R}{Py_2}$ and $OB = \dfrac{R}{Py_1}$.

The slope of iso-revenue line can be derived as follows:

Slope of iso-revenue line $= \dfrac{OA}{OB}$

$$= \dfrac{\dfrac{R}{Py_2}}{\dfrac{R}{Py_1}} = \dfrac{Py_1}{Py_2} = \text{Price ratio}.$$

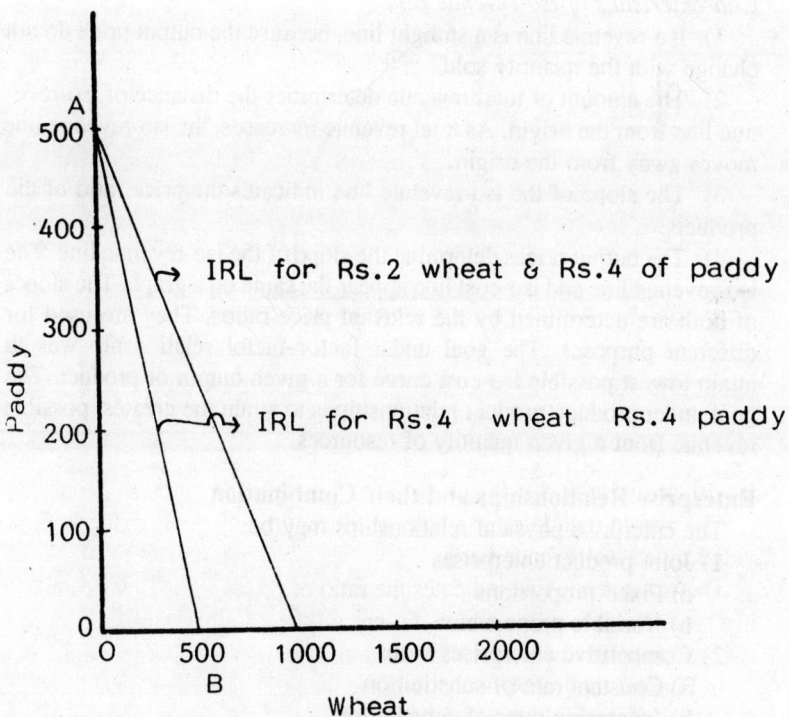

Fig. 4.7. Iso-revenue line for different levels of income.

Iso-revenue Line for Different Levels of Income

The price ratio or the slopes of the price line remains the same so long as relative prices of two products remain the same. The price line will not change their slope and will run parallel to each other.

When the price of wheat is Rs. 2/kg and the price of paddy is Rs. 4/kg, a farmer wishing to obtain a revenue of Rs. 2000 can do so either by producing 1000 kg of wheat or 500 kg of paddy and any combination below these quantities, i.e. with no paddy the revenue is Rs. 1000 × 2 = Rs. 2000 and with no wheat the revenue is Rs. 500 × 4 = Rs. 2000. Connecting these maximum points we will get an iso-revenue line, indicating the possible combinations of two products that can be produced to achieve an equal income. Thus the iso-revenue line provides the choice indicator for economic efficiency of product combinations.

Characteristics of Iso-revenue Line

1) Iso-revenue line is a straight line, because the output price do not change with the quantity sold.

2) The amount of total revenue determines the distance of iso-revenue line from the origin. As total revenue increases, the iso-revenue line moves away from the origin.

3) The slope of the iso-revenue line indicates the price ratio of the products.

4) The output prices determine the slope of the iso-revenue line. The iso-revenue line and iso-cost line appear the same on a graph. The slopes of both are determined by the relevant price ratios. They are used for different purposes. The goal under factor–factor relationship was to attain lowest possible iso-cost curve for a given output of product. The goal under product–product relationship is to attain the greatest possible revenue from a given quantity of resources.

Enterprise Relationships and their Combination

The enterprise physical relationships may be:
1) Joint product enterprises
   a) Fixed proportions
   b) Variable proportions
2) Competitive enterprises with
   a) Constant rate of substitution
   b) Increasing rates of substitution
   c) Decreasing rates of substitution
   d) Other combinations of independent products

3) Complementary enterprises
4) Supplementary enterprises
5) Antagonistic enterprises.

1) JOINT PRODUCT ENTERPRISES

Joint products are produced through a single production process and one of the products cannot be produced alone but must be accompanied by one or more of other products. Either in one form or the other, all agricultural production includes joint products. For example, paddy and straw, mutton and wool, cotton lint and seed, milk and manure from cattle, etc.

Joint products in fixed proportions refer to products which are to be produced only in inflexible proportions. Examples of this nature are found mainly in chemistry. If one molecule of H_2SO_4 is to be produced, it is always by combining two atoms of hydrogen, one atom of sulphur, and four atoms of oxygen.

If the given resources or cost outlay are to be transformed into product, the only choice is one of producing Y_1 and Y_2 products (Fig. 4.8) in the ratio of 2:1 (at *a* 4:2; at *b* 8:4 and at *c* 12:6).

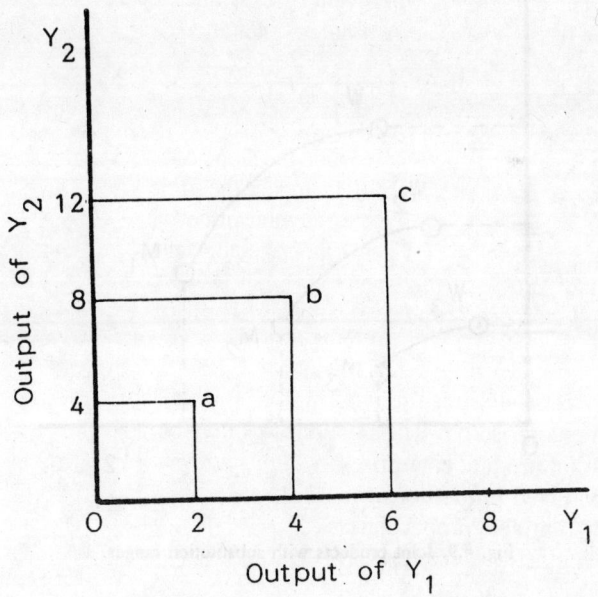

Fig. 4.8. Joint products in fixed proportions.

Joint products with a latitude of substitution are more important in agriculture. Variation in the proportions of joint products from given resources can generally be made in agriculture through changes in breeds and strains, harvesting methods, etc. The choice is not open to produce the different proportions of the joint products. Choice can be made through shifts in the breeds, strains or techniques of production, etc. The opportunity curve for a single level of factor cost is of the nature of W_1 M_1 in Fig. 4.9. Here the mutton can be increased at the expense of wool up to a maximum output of OY_2 and a minimum of OY_1 of wool. However, if wool output with resources held constant is decreased further, output of mutton also decline. Wool output can be less only if mutton output is less. At this point they bear fixed proportion relationship.

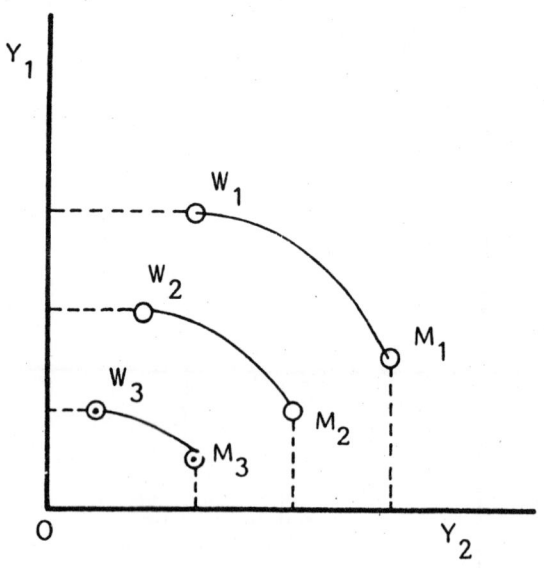

Fig. 4.9. Joint products with substitution ranges.

2) COMPETITIVE ENTERPRISES

Two enterprises are competitive in the use of given resource; if output of one can be increased only through a sacrifice in the production of the other. The nature of enterprise relationship (production possibility curve) is dependent upon the nature of the production function for each independent enterprise.

a) *Constant Rate of Substitution*

Enterprises substituting at constant rate mean, for each one unit increase in one product, a constant amount of another product must be decreased. When the production functions per two or more products are linear (Fig. 4.10), the production possibility curves (opportunity curves) are also linear (Fig. 4.11). A linear opportunity curve indicates that the marginal rates of substitution of one product for the other is at a constant rate.

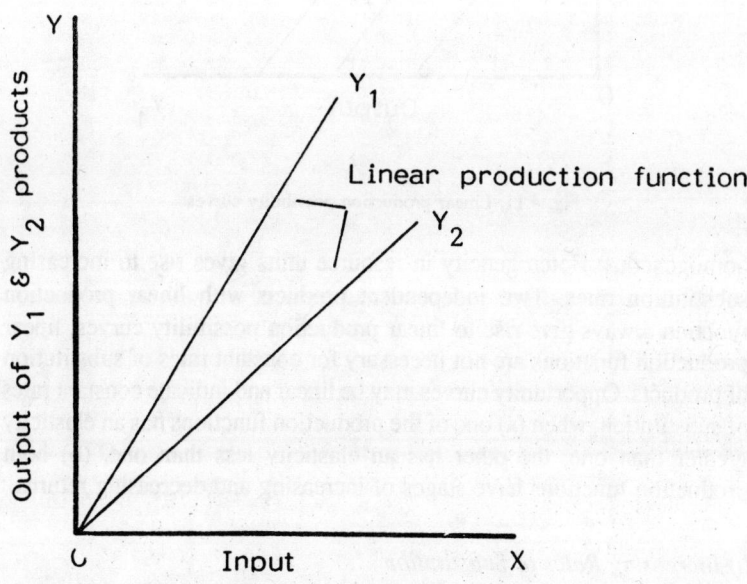

Fig. 4.10. Constant resource productivity.

Constant rates of substitution exists in the presence of linear production functions, only if units of resources shifted back and forth are

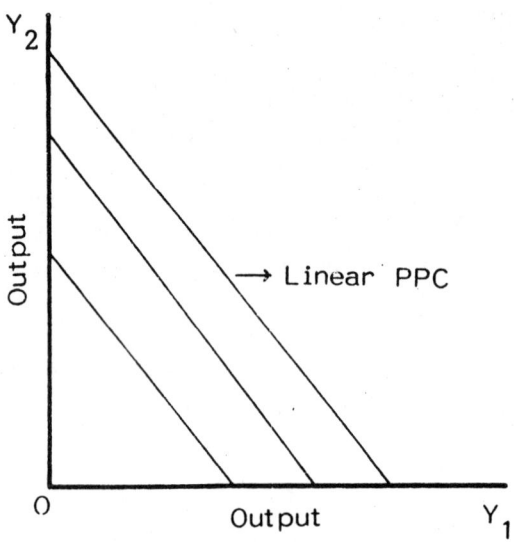

Fig. 4.11. Linear production possibility curves.

homogeneous. Heterogeneity in resource units gives rise to increasing substitution rates. Two independent products with linear production function always give rise to linear production possibility curves, linear production functions are not necessary for constant rates of substitution of products. Opportunity curves may be linear and indicate constant rates of substitution, when (a) one of the production functions has an elasticity greater than one, the other has an elasticity less than one, (b) both production functions have stages of increasing and decreasing returns.

b) Increasing Rates of Substitution

This is the most common relationship between competing independent products. This exists when resources are held constant, successive increases in output of one product bring increasing reduction in the output of the other products. Increasing rates of substitution always hold true when the production function for each independent product is one of decreasing resource productivity (Fig. 4.12). Since substitution between

Y_1 and Y_2 products is at increasing rates, the transformation curve (Fig. 4.13) is concave to the origin (an increasing curvature towards either axis).

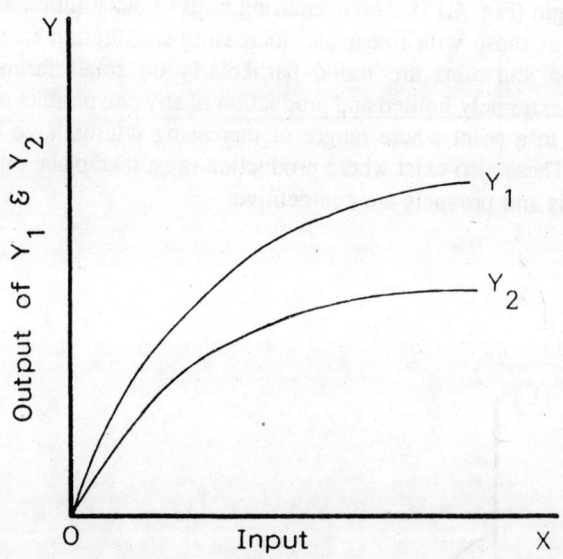

Fig. 4.12. Decreasing resource productivity.

The marginal rates of substitution explain the degree of curvature of production possibility curve. The slope of the curve varies, depending on the quantity of resources to be allocated between two competing products. Increasing rates of substitution in agriculture is due to the following reasons:

   i) Factor–product condition of diminishing marginal productivity.

   ii) Non-homogeneity in quality of limited resources.

   iii) Quasi-supplementary conditions—resources are non-homogeneous in respect to time and concave opportunity curves relate to the seasonality of production. ⋅

c) Decreasing Rates of Substitution

As one product is substituted for another, smaller and smaller sacrifices are made in the latter for each unit increase in the former. Production possibility curves for products produced under conditions of increasing returns give rise to diminishing rates of substitution. Since the elasticity of both the production functions of Y_1 and Y_2 (Fig. 4.14) is greater than one throughout, the rate of substitution necessarily declines as one product is substituted for another and the curve becomes convex to the origin (Fig. 4.15). The decreasing rates of substitution are not as common as those with linear and increasing substitution rates. These production situations are found particularly on small farms, where capital is extremely limited and production of any one product cannot be extended to a point where ranges of increasing returns have been exhausted. These also exist where production must take place on a large-scale basis and products are competitive.

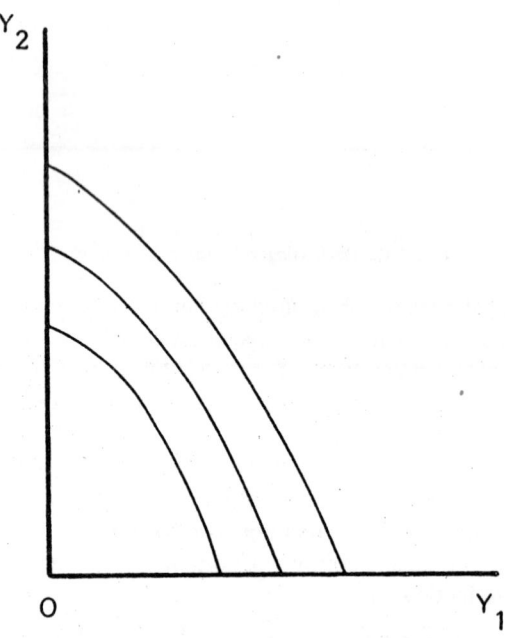

Fig. 4.13. Increasing rates of substitution.

d) Other Combinations of Independent Products

i) Combination of increasing returns product and a constant return product gives a convex opportunity curve (decreasing sacrifice).

ii) When constant return product is compared with a decreasing return product, concave curve results (increasing sacrifice).

iii) Combination of decreasing return product with an increasing return product may give linear, convex or concave curves, depending on the production coefficient for the two products.

iv) Combination of constant return product with one of both increasing and decreasing returns gives an opportunity curve with both convex and concave portions.

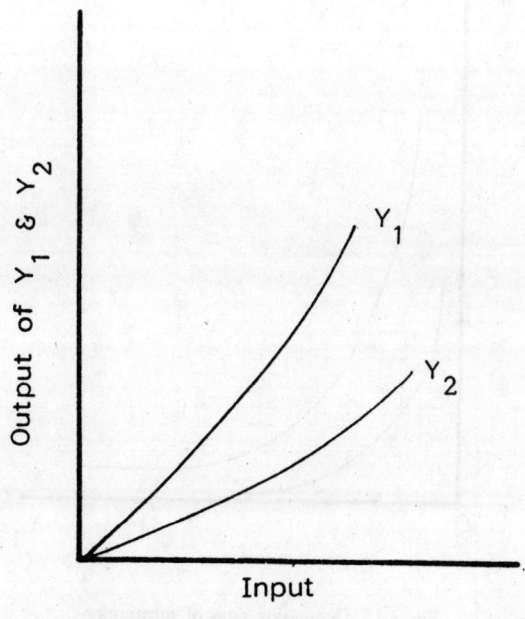

Fig. 4.14. Increasing resource productivity.

3) COMPLEMENTARY ENTERPRISES

Two products are said to be in complementary relationship, when an increase in output of one results in an increase in output of the other, with resource amount held constant. In other words, a shift of resources from a first crop to a second crop, will increase rather than decrease the output of the first. Technical complementarity may arise, because of any one of the three reasons:

a) One enterprise may contribute an element of production—a joint product of the first required by a second enterprise.

b) One enterprise may interact with the other, as the proportions of non-usable joint products change with varying levels of output from a fixed technical unit.

c) One enterprise may divert surplus resources from a second product due to the operation of the law of diminishing returns.

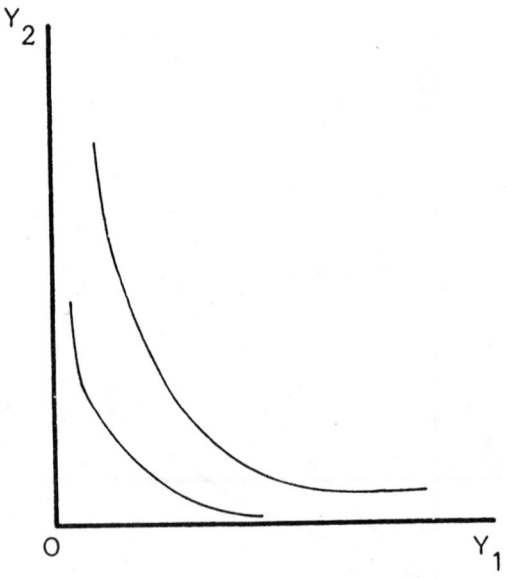

Fig. 4.15. Decreasing rates of substitution.

The first one, is the most important in agriculture; legume and grass crops may contribute elements required in the production of other crops by increasing fertility, improving the soil structure, preventing soil erosion and controlling insects, etc.

Use of resources for the two enterprises makes possible a greater output of one or both, than if each crop were grown independently. For example, paddy crop followed by a pulse crop. Moisture may serve as the element which leads to complementarity. In most of the semi-arid and arid tropics, *kharif* fallowing can be treated simply as a crop, one of the by-products of which is moisture; in areas of tobacco production, a crop such as jowar, or weeds in rotation with tobacco can prove to be complementary by removing the negative element for the tobacco to the extent that they are effective in controlling such diseases as root knot nematodes.

When enterprises are complementary, the production possibility curves are of the general nature as in Figs 4.16 and 4.17.

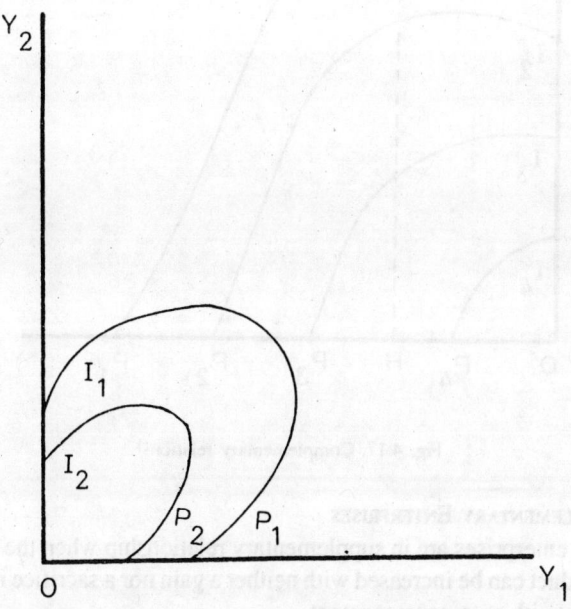

Fig. 4.16. Complementary relationship.

The product Y_1 is complementary with product Y_2 until the production of Y_2 reaches a maximum of *OG* and output of Y_1 reaches *OH*. The products then become competitive and Y_1 substitutes for grain at an increasing rate. A different opportunity curve exists for each level at

which resources are held constant. When mutual complementarity exists
(Y_1 with Y_2 and Y_2 with Y_1), the iso-factor line becomes as indicated in
Fig. 4.18.

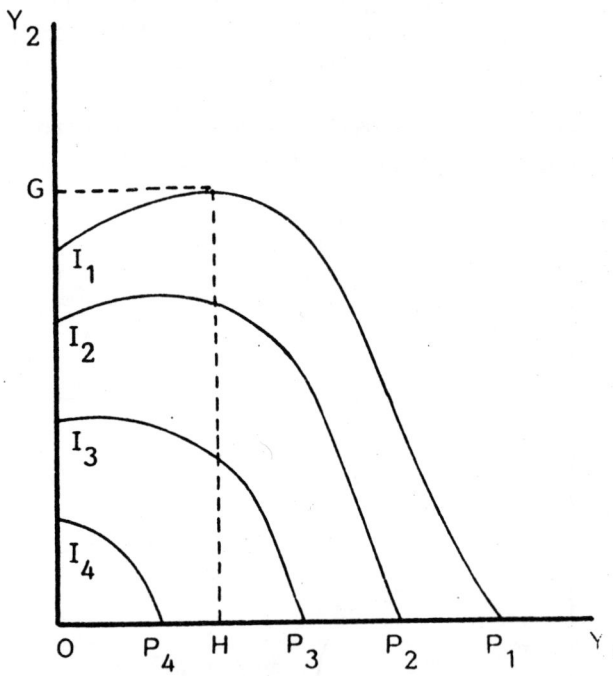

Fig. 4.17. Complementary relationship

4) SUPPLEMENTARY ENTERPRISES

Two enterprises are in supplementary relationship when the output of
one product can be increased with neither a gain nor a sacrifice in another
product, with resources constant.

Supplementary conditions arise mainly out of time and are to be found
especially where:

a) Enterprises can be produced only during a distinct and limited
period of the year.

b) The resources employed give off a flow of services over all time
periods.

When resource services are of the pure stock variety, enterprises concerned are only competitive; when resources employed for one product are in the form of fixed equipment which gives off services irrespective of use in production, these services may be utilised in production through a second product forthcoming in the off-season of the first. The second product does not require a decrease in the output of the first product during its active season, since the flow factor services are generated irrespective of their use in production (non-homogeneity of resource services). Supplementary enterprises may be produced simultaneously, whenever the flow services of resources are concerned and one product does not completely exhaust there.

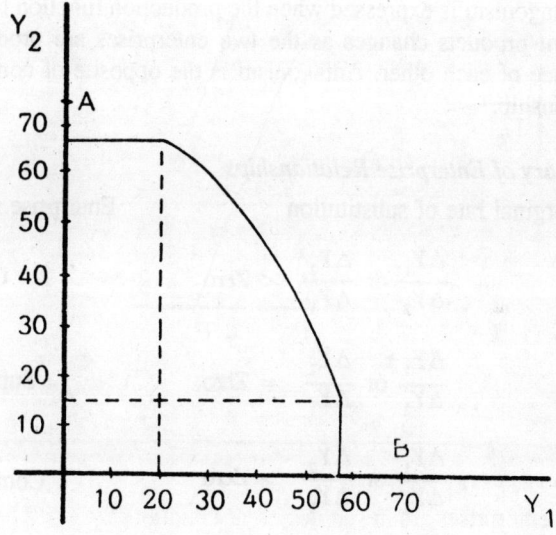

Fig. 4.18. Supplementary relationship.

Period of labour force utilisation in agriculture is seasonal. When it is under-employed, advantage can be taken of this slack labour to engage in livestock or poultry production or off-farm work. Taking part in part-time jobs with little or no effect in the main farm production, this relationship between primary and secondary sources of income is a supplementary one.

The supplementary range is denoted by the linear portions of curve AB and indicates that approximately 20 units of Y_1 can be produced without a sacrifice in Y_2, while roughly 15 units of Y_2 can be produced without a decrease in Y_1.

Beyond linear portions, the transformation function takes on a slope greater than zero and less than infinity and the two commodities are competitive. The resource services which provide the basis for supplementarity between enterprises are not interchangeable in the sense that all units can be withdrawn from one enterprise and used for another. When stock or flow resources cannot be absorbed entirely by one enterprise the possibility of supplementarity exist.

5) ANTAGONISTIC ENTERPRISES

Antagonism is expressed when the production function for two independent products changes as the two enterprises are produced in the presence of each other. Antagonism is the opposite of complementary relationship.

Summary of Enterprise Relationships

Marginal rate of substitution	Enterprise relationship
$\dfrac{\Delta Y_1}{\Delta Y_2}$ or $\dfrac{\Delta Y_2}{\Delta Y_1}$ $< $ Zero	Competitive
$\dfrac{\Delta Y_1}{\Delta Y_2}$ or $\dfrac{\Delta Y_2}{\Delta Y_1}$ $=$ Zero	Supplementary
$\dfrac{\Delta Y_1}{\Delta Y_2}$ or $\dfrac{\Delta Y_2}{\Delta Y_1}$ $>$ Zero	Complementary

If the marginal rate of substitution is less than zero, output of one product must be sacrificed as output of the other is increased and the two products are competitive. If the marginal rate of substitution equal to zero, it indicates that one product can be increased in quantity without a sacrifice in the other, and the two are supplementary. If the substitution ratio is greater than zero, it indicates that an increase or decrease in one product is accompanied by an increase or decrease in the other product and the two enterprises are complementary.

Determination of optimum product combination

The optimum combination of two enterprises with the given resources can be made only if the choice criterion is known. The product price ratios provide the choice indicator for profit maximisation. Maximum profits are attained, with the costs or resources fixed in quantity, when the marginal rate of product substitution is equal to inverse of the product price ratio. In simple algebraic terms, it can be expressed as:

$$\frac{\Delta Y_2}{\Delta Y_1} = \frac{P_{y_1}}{P_{y_2}}.$$

Where $\Delta Y_2 / \Delta Y_1$ is the marginal rate of product substitution and P_{y_1} is the price of Y_1 and P_{y_2} is the price of Y_2 product.

The above criterion can also be written as: $(\Delta Y_1)(P_{y_1}) = (P_{y_2})(\Delta Y_2)$. This equation states that with resources allocated to maximise profits, the marginal value product of a unit of resource allocated to Y_1 is equal to the marginal value product of a unit of resource allocated to Y_2.

When $\quad \dfrac{\Delta Y_2}{\Delta Y_1} < \dfrac{P_{y_1}}{P_{y_2}} \quad$ Profits can be increased by substituting Y_1 for Y_2.

When $\quad \dfrac{\Delta Y_2}{\Delta Y_1} > \dfrac{P_{y_1}}{P_{y_2}} \quad$ Profits can be increased by substituting Y_2 for Y_1.

The optimum product combination can be achieved when the slope of the iso-revenue line (Fig. 4.19), and the slope of the production possibility curves are equal. Or where the iso-revenue line is tangential to the production possibility curve, the two slopes are equal and therefore it is the point of optimum product combination.

Substitution of Y_1 for Y_2 is always profitable, as long as the slope of the opportunity curve is less than the slope of the iso-revenue. Substitution of Y_2 for Y_1 is always profitable when the opportunity line is greater than the slope of the iso-revenue line. At the point of tangency, the ratio of marginal cost of two products is equal to the ratio of their marginal value products.

TABULAR METHOD

The other method is to calculate the net revenue from many combinations and locate the one which promises highest returns.

Ex: When 700 units of X are used P_{y_1} = Rs. 7/Q; P_{y_2} = Rs. 10/Q.

Table 4.4. Determination of optimum product combination

Y_1	Y_2	ΔY_1	ΔY_2	$\Delta Y_2/\Delta Y_1$	$P_{y_1} \cdot Y_1$	$P_{y_2} \cdot Y_2$	Total revenue
0	78				0	780	780
10	76	10	2	2/10 = 0.2	70	760	830
20	72	10	4	= 0.4	140	720	860
30	67	10	5	= 0.5	210	670	880
40	60	10	7	= 0.7	280	600	880
50	48	10	12	= 1.2	350	480	830
60	28	10	20	= 2.0	420	280	700
70	0	10	28	= 2.8	490	0	490

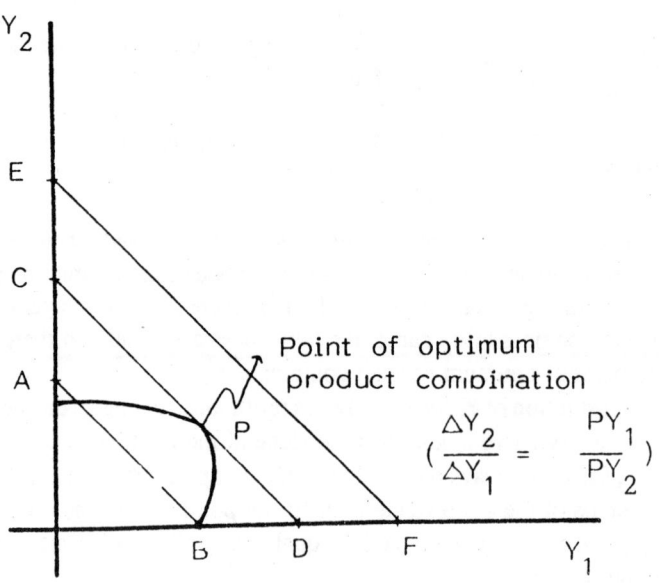

Fig. 4.19. Optimum product–product combination.

Computations of the maximum revenue combination of two products Y_1 and Y_2 for 700 units of X are given in Table 4.4. When price of Y_2 is

Rs. 10/qtl and price of Y_1 is Rs. 7/qtl, the maximum revenue combination of products is 40 units of Y_1 and 60 units of Y_2. The total revenue is Rs. 880 at this point.

$$\frac{\Delta Y_2}{\Delta Y_1} < \frac{P_{Y_1}}{P_{Y_2}}$$

$$\frac{7}{10} = \frac{7}{10}$$

$$0.7 = 0.7.$$

RIDGE LINES AND ISOCLINE

Ridge lines can be used to separate the range of product competition from ranges of complementarity. The ridge lines are also called border lines. Ridge lines are also called isoclines, since the slope of the iso-resource curves are identical at the point of intersection.

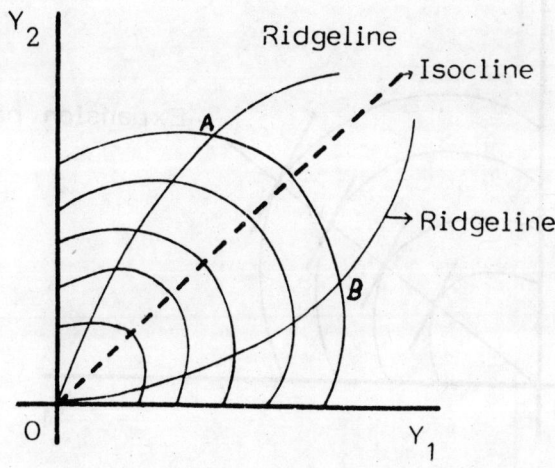

Fig. 4.20. Ridge lines and iso-clines.

In Fig. 4.20, line *OA* and *OB* are called ridge lines. Line *OA* intersects production possibility curves (PPC) where they are horizontal and line *OB* intersects where the curve go vertical. On line *OA*, MRPS of Y_1 for

Y_2 is infinity and on line OB the MRPS of Y_1, for Y_2 is zero. Portions of production possibility curves within the border lines, have negative slope, indicating competition. Portions outside the border lines have positive slope indicating complementarity.

EXPANSION PATH IN PRODUCT–PRODUCT ANALYSIS

As increasing amounts of resources become available, a cultivator may wish to expand output. The pattern of expansion which would be followed can be indicated by an expansion line. This line is derived by joining up all the points of tangency (A,B,C,D) between the iso-revenue lines and the production possibility curves (Fig 4.21).

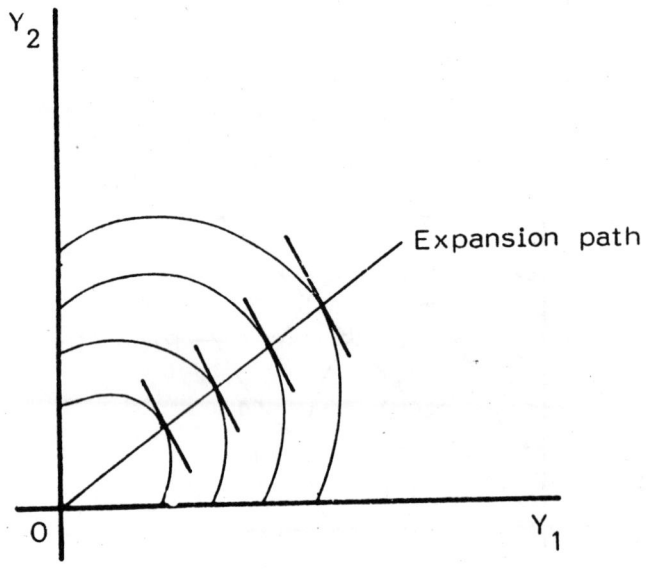

Fig. 4.21. Expansion path.

At all points on the expansion path, $\dfrac{\Delta Y_2}{\Delta Y_1} = \dfrac{P_{Y_1}}{P_{Y_2}}$

The high profit point is located somewhere, along with expansion path specified by the points of tangency, with the prices indicated by the iso-revenue lines.

Returns to Scale

Economic theory gives two types of factor–product relationship in a production function.

1) Proportionality relationship
2) Scale relationship

In contrast to proportionality relationship, scale relationship refers to a simultaneous increase in all resources. Proportionality relationships involve the short-run production functions, of which one or more factors are fixed. Scale relationships involve long-run production functions, of which no factors are fixed. When all factors are increased in fixed proportion, they in effect represent one single aggregate resource; this aggregate of resources can be considered as a single homogeneous factor, since particular factors are combined in the same ratio irrespective of output.

The laws of return are often confused with 'returns to scale'. It is meant that the behaviour of production or returns, when all the production factors are increased or decreased simultaneously, in the same ratio.

In other words, in returns to scale, we analyse the effect of doubling, trebling or multiples of all inputs of productive resources on the output of the product.

In returns to scale (Table 4.5), necessary factors of production are increased or decreased to the same extent, so that whatever the scale of production, the proportion among the factors remains the same. The output do not increase or decrease strictly according to the change in the scale, but one can observe the same three stages, i.e. increasing returns (product increases by greater proportion), constant returns (product increases by same proportion) and decreasing returns (product increases by a smaller proportion).

In actual situations, the scale of production cannot be increased beyond a certain unit. Hence the law of diminishing returns also operates in returns to scale. In practice it is the law of variable proportions, which has universal application. Scale relationships reflected only if all factors are held in constant proportions as output increased.

Pure Scale Relationships

We consider the production function of the nature, where all resources are variable.

$$Y = f(X_1, X_2, X_3, X_4, ..., X_n)$$

Pure scale relationships are involved only if all resources which go into production are increased by the same proportion, i.e. if one input is doubled, the input of all others must be doubled. If all resources are increased, but some are doubled while other are tripled, the resulting change in input–output relationships involve variable proportions.

Table 4.5. Returns to scale

S.No.	Scale (Acres + workers)	Total product (qtl)	Marginal product in qtl
1	1 + 3	2	2 stage I increasing returns
2	2 + 6	5	3
3	3 + 9	9	4
4	4 +12	14	5
5	5 +15	19	5 stage II constant returns
6	6 +18	24	5
7	7 +21	28	4 stage III decreasing returns
8	8 +24	31	3
9	9 +27	33	2

Scale relationships are indicated by lines OS_1 and OS_2 in Fig. 4.22. The scale line is drawn in linear fashion to indicate that factors are held in fixed proportions. Scale relationships are indicated by the intersection of lines OS_1 or OS_2 with the product contours. At the point of intersection of OS_2 with the 100 unit contour, the factor inputs include 30 of X_1 and 40 of X_2. A doubling of factors extends to 60 of X_1 and 80 of X_2. The product contour which intersects this point on the scale line denotes an output of 200 units of X_2. Thus constant returns to scale holds true as an increase in factor input by 100 per cent has increased output by the same percentage. When the factors increased to 90 of X_1 and 120 of X_2. it results in an increase of product to 300 (50 per cent increase in factor and product and the elasticity is again 1.0). The contour map of Fig. 4.22 denotes a linear, homogeneous production function. Decreasing returns to scale are illustrated in Fig. 4.23, when X_1 and X_2 are held constant in proportions, as indicated by scale line S_d. The percentage increase in aggregate input is greater than the percentage increase in output of product. The successive distances of scale segment are larger and larger and the position of product contour (iso-quants) move farther apart for 100, 200 and 300 units. If output is to be increased from 100 to 200 or by 100 per cent, aggregate factor input must be more than doubled; the distance *ab* is greater than *OC*, showing that diminishing returns to scale holds true.

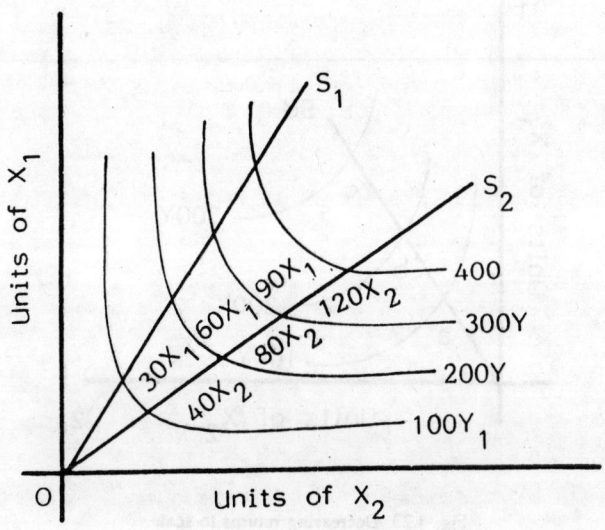

Fig. 4.22. Constant returns to scale.

In increasing returns to scale, successive distances of scale segment are becoming smaller and smaller and the position of iso-quants is coming closer and closer (Fig. 4.24).

Returns to scale is frequently measured by fitting the least square Cobb-Douglas production function to input–output data and then adding up the exponents, which are production elasticities of the inputs. If the sum is less than unity then it is decreasing returns; if greater than unity, it is increasing returns and if equal to unity, it is constant returns. Consider the production function

$$Y = ax_1^{b_1} \cdot x_2^{b_2} \cdot x_3^{b_3} \cdot - \cdot X_n^{b_n}$$

Y = Total output

X_1 = Land input

X_2 = Fertiliser input
X_3 = Labour input
X_n = Other inputs

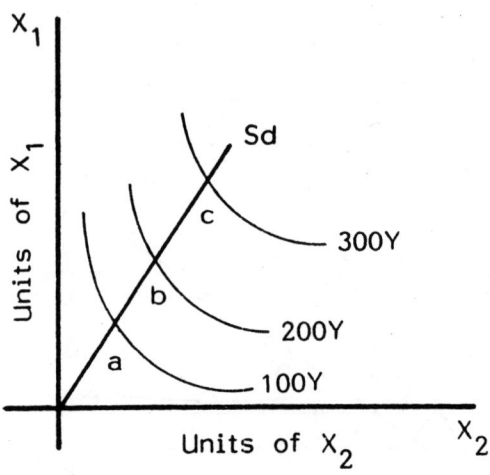

Fig. 4.23. Decreasing returns to scale.

The returns to land as a physical input are given by the coefficient b_1, accordingly to fertiliser b_2, to labour b_3 and for input X_n, coefficient is b_n. The returns to scale from this function are given by the summation of individual elasticities of coefficients, i.e.

$$\text{Returns to scale} = \sum_{i=1}^{n} b_i .$$

Thus decreasing, constant and increasing returns to scale are indicated accordingly as this sum is less than, equal to, or greater than unity, respectively. This relationship explained pertains only to the Cobb-Douglas production function.

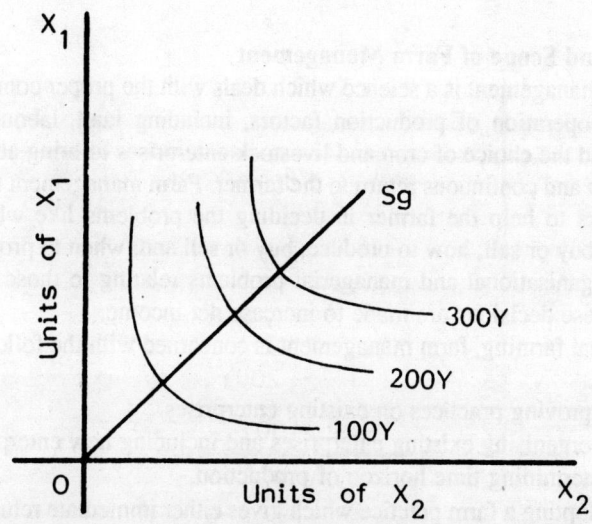

Fig. 4.24. Increasing returns to scale.

CHAPTER 5

Farm Management

Nature and Scope of Farm Management

Farm management is a science which deals with the proper combination and operation of production factors, including land, labour and capital and the choice of crop and livestock enterprises to bring about a maximum and continuous return to the farmer. Farm management therefore, seeks to help the farmer in deciding the problems like what to produce, buy or sell; how to produce, buy or sell and; when to produce, and in organisational and managerial problems relating to those decisions. These decisions are made to increase net income.

In actual farming, farm management is concerned with the following problems.

1) Improving practices on existing enterprises.

2) Reorganising existing enterprises and including new enterprises.

3) Determining time horizon of production.

4) Adopting a farm practice which gives either immediate returns or long-term returns.

5) Deciding the best size of farm.

6) Deciding capital goods required and labour to be hired.

7) Marketing problems including in what forms, when, where and at what terms to buy inputs and sell output.

8) Expectation of factor input and product prices.

9) Credit requirement and sources of credit.

DEFINITIONS

Farm management is that branch of Agricultural Economics, which deals with the business principles and practices of farming with an object of obtaining the maximum possible returns from the farm as an unit under a sound farming programme.

Warren: Farm management is the study of the business principles of farming. "It may be defined as the science of organisation and the management of the farm enterprise for the purpose of securing the greatest continuous profit".

Efferson: "Farm management is the science which considers the organisation and operation of the farm from the point of view of efficiency and continuous profit".

Adams: "Farm management as the method is the utilisation of sound principles in the selection, organisation and conduct of an individual farm business for the purpose of obtaining the greatest possible profits".

Bradford and Johnson: "Farm management is a branch of Agricultural Economics, which deals with wealth earning and wealth spending activities of a farmer, in relation to the organisation and operation of the individual farm unit for securing the maximum possible net income".

SCOPE OF FARM MANAGEMENT

Farm management is generally considered to be microeconomic in scope. It deals with the allocation of resources at the farm level of an individual farm. It is in a way interlinked with the problem of resource allocation in the agricultural sector, or even in the economy as a whole. The primary concern of farm management is the farm as an unit.

It covers all aspects of farming, which have a bearing on the economic efficiency of the farm. Thus the types of enterprises to be combined, the types of crops to be grown, the dosage of fertilisers to be applied, the types of implements to be used, the way the farm operations are to be carried out, the manner in which continuous farm profits are obtained — all these fall within the purview of farm management.

Management Decisions

It is seen that farm management is called the science of decision making or a science of choice. It is a choice in the efficient utilisation of the available but limited farm resources among competing ends. These decisions are made at the farm level. The principal farm management decisions to be made by most of the farmers are:

1) Strategic Management Decisions

a) Deciding the best size of the farm: type of farming area, types of business, land under irrigation, mechanisation, ability of the farmer to manage, .tc.

b) Decisions on farm labour and machinery programmes.

c) Decisions on construction of building.

d) Decisions regarding irrigation, conservation and reclamation programmes.

2) Operational Management Decisions

In the day-to-day operations of the farm business, the frequency of these decisions is more as compared to strategic management decisions, but the investment involved is relatively small and impact short lived. These decisions are generally as follows:

What do produce?	Selection of enterprises.
How much to produce?	Enterprise-mix.
How to produce?	Selection of least cost-efficient methods,
When to produce?	timing of production.

3) Administrative Decisions

a) Financing the farm business.

b) Supervision of work.

c) Accounting and book keeping.

d) Adjustments to government programmes and policies.

e) Production for home consumption and the market.

4) Marketing Decisions

a) Buying—when to buy, where to buy and how to buy the farm inputs.

b) Selling—when, where and how to sell farm products.

Farm Management in Relation to other Science

Agronomy: For developing physical input–output relationships in crop production, fertiliser, irrigation use, etc.

Chemistry: The knowledge of composition, structure and deficiencies of soils and the ways and means of improving the soils and their productivity.

Botany: Supplies knowledge of crops, crop varieties and their ecology.

Plant breeding: Provides the knowledge of seeds and their varieties.

Agricultural Engineering: Provides knowledge pertaining to the use of machinery, power and equipment and their efficiency.

Animal Husbandry: Knowledge of animal feeding and maintenance and breeding.

Sociology: Understanding cultural traits, community environment and social forces in relation to agricultural enterprises and farm groups.

Psychology: Provides information on human motivation and attitudes towards new techniques of agricultural production and their adoption.

Farm Management and Production Economics

The tools and techniques for farm management are supplied by the general economic theory. Farm management is an integral part of production economics. It is often difficult to make a distinction between the two. It is generally accepted that while farm management is concerned with economic efficiency at the farm level, agricultural production economics deals with allocative efficiency in resources in agriculture as a whole.

Thus farm management is an intra-farm study, production economics is an inter-farm study.

Farm Management Problems in India

1. Subsistence type of farming and more family oriented farms: Farm as a household.
2. Predominance of small farms—small size of farm business.
3. Transitory stage from traditional farming to scientific and commercial farms.
4. Regional variations in farm practices, productivity and cost structure and thereby farm incomes.
5. Improved technology and adoption to location specific problems, slow adoption of innovations.
6. Major farming resources—human and bullock labour, crop, land and irrigation water are available in a combination—labour plentiful and capital scarce.
7. Under-employment and unemployment.
8. Lack of communication systems and regulated market organisations stand as major bottlenecks.

From the farm management viewpoint, optimising resource use calls for:

1) Fuller use of more plentiful resources specially labour.
2) More intensive use of land and water, since all of India is in tropics and subtropics, where year-round cropping is possible.
3) Adding operating capital and technical inputs in careful combination to maximise their benefits, while economising their use.
4) Developing suitable farm plans, to obtain continuous higher net incomes to the farmers.

History of farm management in India

Farm management development is of recent origin. Early period of farm management development was by agronomists and soil scientists.

The work mostly involved descriptions of farming methods, practices and structure of farm organisation.

Scanty attention was given to economic aspects of farm management. No systematic farm management studies was undertaken in the earlier days. First organised study in the field of farm cost accounting was initiated in 1923–24 by the Punjab Board of Economic Inquiry. The board has since been providing a good deal of information of regional importance on costs, returns and resource use pattern in farming.

An exhaustive study on farm management was made by Prof. P.C. Patil, Professor of Agricultural Economics, Poona, during 1928–30. The investigations were carried out in six districts of Bombay presidency. The first All-India study of costs and returns on farmers holdings was conducted by the Indian Council of Agricultural Research (ICAR) during 1933–36. The study was limited to the costs of production of sugarcane and cotton and other important crops in the principal sugarcane growing tracts of India. The data and the findings were published under the title *Report on the cost of the production of crops in principal sugarcane and cotton tracts in India*, 1939.

The research programme committee, Planning Commission, Government of India, initiated studies in the economics of farm management in six regions of the country—Punjab, Uttar Pradesh, Madhya Pradesh, Madras, Bombay and West Bengal in 1954–55 to 1956–57 for a period of three years. The studies were extended to Andhra Pradesh, Bihar, and Orissa in 1957–58. The reports on an All-India basis gave a deep insight into the agricultural economy of the country. The scheme on the Cost of Production of Principal Crops in different states was sponsored by the Directorate of Economics and Statistics in 1970–71.

The Agro-Economic Research Centres established in 1954–55 for different regions are working on various aspects of rural economy as well as on price movements and fair price shops. The reports provide good material for policy decisions. Further, various agricultural universities and social sciences research institutions are presently engaged on research in farm management problems and farm cost studies in different locations.

Evaluation of Farm Management through Economic Principles Applied in Farm Management

Basically farm management is the application of agricultural sciences and economic principles to the organisation and operation of a farm business. Farm management principles serve as a guideline for collecting and using requisite information for rational decision making. They also provide a set of tools for the preparation of farm budgets and production programmes.

The following are the seven basic principles involved in making rational decisions.

1) Principle of variable proportions or laws of returns.
2) Cost principle.
3) Principle of substitution between inputs.
4) Principle of substitution between products.
5) Principle of equi-marginal returns or opportunity cost principle.
6) Principle of comparative advantage.
7) Time comparison principle.

1) PRINCIPLE OF VARIABLE PROPORTIONS

This principle helps in making decisions, such as:

a) The level to which yield per acre, milk per cow, etc., should be pushed to secure maximum profit.

b) The size of the farm one should operate with the given resources of capital, labour and management.

c) The amount of fertiliser, labour or type of machinery one should use.

This relationship is determined by the law of variable proportions. This is explained with the help of Table 5.1. The fertiliser data obtained from a farm in West Godavari district of Andhra Pradesh is used for this purpose. The output of paddy (var. Vasistha) depends upon the application of nitrogen input and other inputs are held constant. The farmer can determine the most profitable level of nitrogen use (or on the other hand he can also decide simultaneously the economic amount of paddy output) by equating the marginal product to the input–output price ratio, i.e. $\frac{\Delta Y}{\Delta X} = \frac{P_x}{P_y}$. In this table, the price of paddy (P_y) is Rs. 0.84/kg and price of nitrogen resource (P_x) is Rs. 4.02. Then the most profitable level of nitrogen use is obtained at 36 kg/ha (between 30 and 40 units) by applying the above principle. If the farmer uses more than this, the marginal value derived is Rs. 5.04 and the marginal cost of fertiliser is Rs. 40.2. Thus the farmer has to incur loss to the extent of Rs. 35 and further extension of nitrogen will bring less and less marginal returns than the factor cost. The farmer should desist from applying more than 36 kg of nitrogen. He can go on applying nitrogen up to 36 kg, as it adds more value than the factor cost.

Table 5.1. Physical and economic efficiency of resource application

Nitrogen input (kg/ha)	Estimated yield of rice (kg/ha)	Additional input (ΔX)	Additional output (ΔY)	Marginal productivity (ΔY/ΔX)	Marginal cost (MC) Rs.	Total cost (TC), Rs.	Total returns (TR), Rs.	Marginal returns (MR), Rs.	Net returns (NR), Rs.
0	4,437					0	3,727.08		3,727.08
10	4,648	10	211	21.1	40.2	40.2	2,904.32	177.24	3,864.3
20	4,809	10	161	16.9	40.2	80.4	4,039.56	135.24	3,959.16
30	4,918	10	109	10.9	40.2	120.6	4,131.12	91.56	4,010.52
40	4,976	10	58	5.8	40.2	160.8	4,179.84	48.72	4,019.04
50	4,982	10	6	0.6	40.2	200.1	4,187.40	5.04	3,987.30
60	4,937	10	-45	-4.5	40.2	240.12	4,147.08	-37.8	3,906.96
70	4,842	10	-95	-9.5	40.2	280.14	4,067.28	-79.8	3,787.14
80	4,695	10	-147	-14.7	40.2	320.16	3,943.80	-123.48	3,623.64

Thus, (i) if the marginal unit of nitrogen yields less value than its price, nitrogen use can be reduced, (ii) if the application of further units of nitrogen yields more value than the cost of nitrogen, its use can be increased and (iii) its use can be stopped when the value of additional product equals to the added cost of nitrogen.

Figure 5.1 drawn from the data in Table 5.1 depicts, operation of the law of diminishing returns differs from the classical theoretical curves as shown in Fig. 2.4 of Chapter 2. The total product curve is increasing and reaches maximum and then starts to decline. The marginal product curve continuously shows diminishing trend, which indicates the farmer is operating in stage-(ii) of production and the total product is increasing. Once the marginal product touches x- axis and falls below zero, the production process has entered stage-(iii) and total produce starts to decline from its maximum.. Hence the relevant stage where the producer should operate is decided before the marginal product falls to less than zero.

The principle of diminishing returns is otherwise known as the principle of added costs and added returns.

2) Application of the Fixed and Variable Costs Principle

In order to maximise net revenue, variable (or added) costs are relevant costs to be considered. In this context, profit rules for decisions in the long-run and short-run planning period can be described as under.

In the short-run, gross returns must cover the variable costs. The maximum net revenue is obtained when marginal cost equals the price of the product.

$$MC = MR$$

If the gross returns are less than total costs, but are still larger than the variable costs, guiding principle should be to keep increasing production as long as added returns (MR) are greater than added costs.

In the short run, MC = MR point may be at a level of input use, which may involve a loss instead of profit, yet, at this point loss will be minimised. In such a situation, objective should be to minimise losses in the short run. This situation of operating the farms when price of MR is greater than average variable cost but less than the average total cost is common in agriculture. This explains why farmers do as they do; why they keep farming even when they run into losses.

The selling price must therefore, be greater than the variable cost of producing each unit of product in the short-run, if farming is to be carried on. Over long period, however, selling price must be greater than the variable cost and fixed cost per unit. Once these costs are covered, farm entrepreneur will not be interested in the coverage of per unit cost of production. The marginal or added cost of each increase in production will then be important in determining how far he should go. It will be seldom economical to produce with the lowest per-unit cost. The point of lowest average cost is not necessarily the point of lowest marginal cost and even lowest marginal cost is not the optimum point. The optimum point will be where added returns are equal to the added cost. However, the optimum point can be at the point of lowest per-unit cost, only in a case where the minimum cost coincides with the maximum profit output. This is the case when the selling price or marginal revenue are equal to minimum cost.

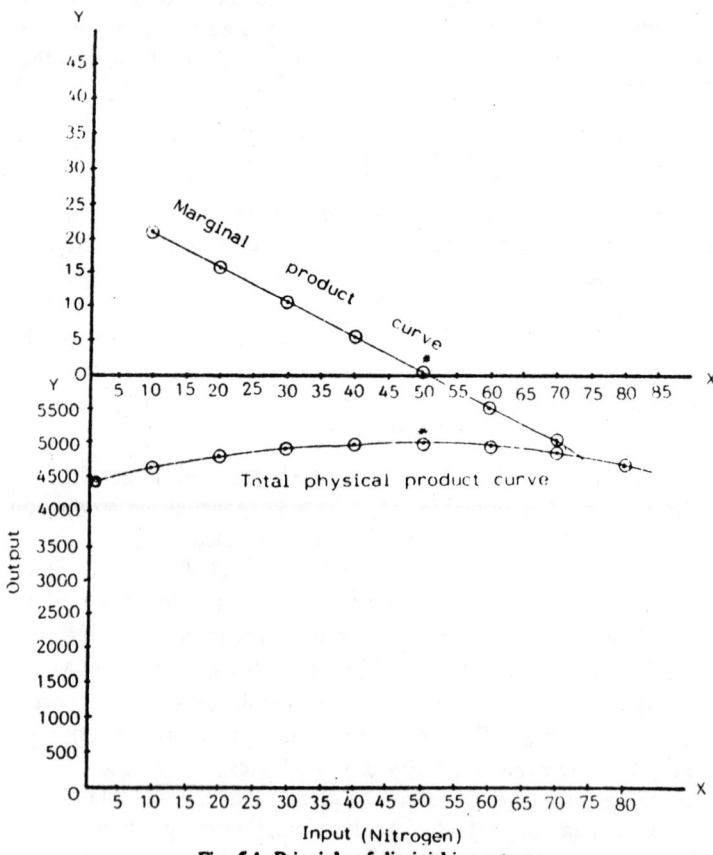

Fig. 5.1. **Principle of diminishing returns.**

Take for example an actual farm situation—as given in the Table 5.2. In column two Rs. 4000 are shown as gross returns against a total cost of Rs. 1300, giving net returns of Rs. 2700. Suppose the prices of product decline low to one-fourth prices, gross returns would be Rs. 1000. If costs remain the same at Rs. 1300 there would be a loss of Rs. 300. But it will still be profitable to keep operating the farm business, because if farm is not operating, the fixed cost of Rs. 1000 will be loss. If the farm is operated, the gross income of Rs. 1000 exceeds the variable cost of Rs. 300 by Rs. 700; on account of this fixed costs get reduced. Here the farmer is minimising the loss (Rs. 300 only instead of Rs. 1000 by operating the farm), i.e. the Rs. 700 left over after meeting the variable costs (Rs. 300) will be compensated in the fixed costs Rs. 1000 and the actual loss is only Rs. 300. If the farm does not operate the farmer has to loose the whole of fixed cost of Rs. 1000. By operating the farm the loss is minimised to Rs. 300.

The added or marginal quantities are more important than total cost or fixed costs. Certain variable costs when incurred or committed become fixed costs (sowing of seed, labour, irrigation).

Table 5.2. An illustration of maximising profits and minimising losses on a farm

		Rs.
a) Total fixed costs	....	1000
b) Total variable costs	....	300
c) Total costs (FC + VC)	....	1300
d) Gross returns	....	4000
e) Net returns	....	2700

The typical farmers do not have unlimited capital. They must employ related economic criteria in specifying the optimum quantity of variable factor to be used per unit of fixed factor. In case the input–output relationship involves only decreasing returns and fixed costs are not involved, the minimum quantity of input to be used is zero. Only when the price of the product is sufficiently large relative to the price of the factor, the quantity of factor should be used is more than zero.

If the fixed costs are involved, the minimum quantity of input which should be used differs from zero, even if the input–output relationship includes only diminishing returns. The minimum amount of input to be used is defined by the total cost and total revenue from the use of the factor. The total costs and total revenue are related to use of a variable factor in Fig. 5.2.

The minimum quantity of input is OX_1 with fixed costs at OC, and if the price of the product is sufficiently low, none of the factor should be used. If the total revenue curve is lower throughout than the total cost curve for the resource none of the factor should be used.

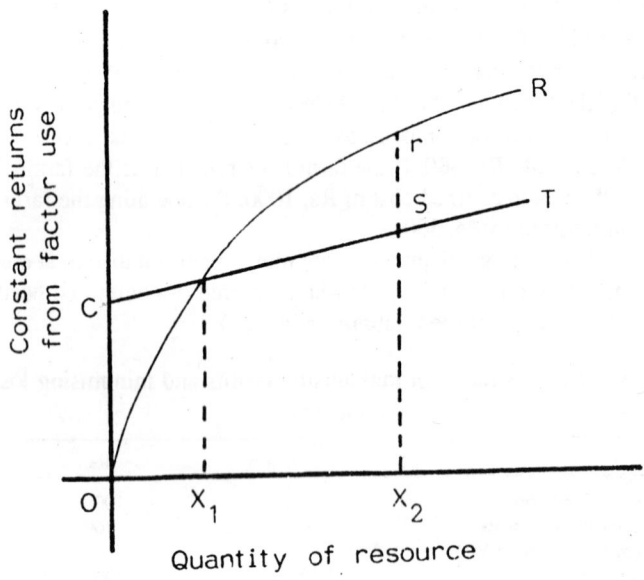

Fig. 5.2. Total revenue and total cost of using a variable resource in relation to minimum and maximum quantities of input.

If the product price is sufficiently high relative to the factor price, the minimum quantity of factor which should be used is OX_1. For inputs larger than this, revenue exceeds costs and net profit is generated. Profit from the fixed factor can be increased until input reaches the magnitude of OX_2.

This is the level which maximises profit for the fixed producing unit. At OX_2 the difference between total revenue and total cost (rs.) is at a maximum. At this input level, marginal cost and marginal revenue from using the resource are equal, as denoted by the slopes of the two curves R and T. The optimum input quantity for a farmer with limited capital and other profitable investment opportunities will fall somewhere between OX_1 and OX_2.

3) LAW OF EQUIMARGINAL RETURNS

If a farmer had access to any amount of working capital and labour and could expand his acreage and building facilities, etc., as far as he wished, he would not have any difficulty in deciding which commodities to produce, he would not even compare one enterprise with another. Instead he would produce all crops and livestock products physically possible in his locality, considering weather, climate, soil and other physical factors. The decision rule would be simple, select all products which can be produced and expand output as long as the added returns are greater than added costs.

But choice on the number and size of enterprises in this manner cannot be made, because resources are limited. Expansion of one enterprise or practice generally requires an equivalent contribution in another. The question is, "which enterprise or combination of enterprises will give the greatest income"? Such an optimum choice of enterprises is made based on the 'principle of equimarginal returns' or the 'principle of opportunity costs'.

This law states that profits are maximised by using a resource in such a way, that the marginal returns from that resource are equal in all cases.

Table 5.3. Estimated total and added yields of rice (kg/ha)

	Goutami		Vasistha		Pankaj	
	Total	Added	Total	Added	Total	Added
0	4,458	244	4,437	211	4,653	
10	4,702	204	4,648	161	4,818	165
20	4,906	164	4,809	109	4,953	136
30	5,070	124	4,918	58	5,059	105
40	5,194	84	4,976	6	5,135	75
50	5,278	45	4,982	−45	5,182	47
60	5,323	4	4,937	−95	5,200	18
70	5,327	−36	4,842	−147	5,188	−12
80	5,291		4,695		5,146	−42

A farmer has Rs. 320 for the purchase of nitrogen fertiliser for applying to three varieties of rice, viz. Gautami, Vasistha and Pankaj. The problem is, how much amount of this limited capital should be spent on each variety to obtain highest profit?

Table 5.4. Most profitable level of nitrogen use in three rice varieties

Nitrogen per ha (kg)	Added nitrogen (kg)	Cost of added nitrogen (Rs.)	Value of added yield of paddy (Rs.)		
			Gautami	Vasistha	Pankaj
0	10	40	195.20	168.80	132.00
10	10	40	163.20	128.80	108.00
20	10	40	131.20	87.20	84.80
30	10	40	99.20	46.40	60.80
40	10	40	67.20	4.80	37.60
50	10	40	36.00	−36.00	14.40
60	10	40	3.20	−76.00	−9.60
70	10	40	−28.80	−117.60	−33.60
80					

Cost of N @ Rs.4/kg and paddy @ Re. 0.80/kg.

If the farmer follows the law of average returns he gets a net profit of Rs. 666.40 on Gautami (Table 5.3). If the farmer follows the principle of added returns and added costs, the most profitable levels of nitrogen application for each rice variety are as follows (Table 5.4):

50 kg of N for Gautami,

40 kg of N for Vasistha and

40 kg of N for Pankaj.

The farmer needs 130 kg of nitrogen for all the three varieties. But the availability of capital with the farmer is limited to the extent of Rs. 320, that means he can purchase only 80 kg of N at the rate of Rs. 4/kg of N. The problem is, how he should allocate Rs. 320 or 80 kg of N to all the three variet's to maximise net income?

Table 5.5. Allocation of nitrogen among the three varieties of rice based on the law of equimarginal returns

Dose of nitrogen	Variety	Addition to income (Rs.)
I	Gautami	195.20
II	Vasistha	168.80
III	Gautami	163.20
IV	Pankaj	132.00
V	Gautami	131.20
VI	Vasistha	128.80
VII	Pankaj	108.00
VIII	Gautami	92.20
Total 80 kg N		1126.40

The farmer has to follow the principle of equimarginal returns to allocate 80 kg of N to the three varieties of rice as shown in Table 5.5. By following the allocation as per the principle of equimarginal returns, the farmer will get a total income of Rs. 1126.40. Any alteration in the schedule different from that shown in Table 5.5 will not result in increased income. Therefore, it is the added returns from each dose of the resource that will bring maximum income but not the average returns that guides the resource allocation of limited resources.

Law of Equi-marginal Returns versus Added Cost-added Returns Principle

Both the laws are closely associated with the law of diminishing returns. But their application depends upon the availability of the capital input. When capital is limited, the farmer must obviously stop short of its application to the level where MC = MR. He is handicapped to follow the added cost-added return principle, because if he uses more of it in one enterprise, there will be equivalent decrease in its use for other enterprises, with the result that profit cannot be maximised. As against this situation, where capital is unlimited, profit is maximised when its application is extended to the level where MC = MR – the essence of the added cost-added return principle.

What is the Practical Utility of the Law of Equi-marginal Returns

a) It guides the farmer to plan his budget for the preparation of his cropping scheme and fitting there in his livestock programme.

b) It enables him to determine enterprise relationship—complementary or competitive.

c) It provide guidance to the adoption of diversified or specialised farming, as there is a profitable limit for each enterprises as well as most profitable enterprise.

This principle is also called as the law of opportunity cost, which is defined as "the cost of using one resource in production of one product is the return that would have been received from the same resource used in its most profitable alternative use".

The principle refers to the money returns or advantage which might have been obtained from any factor used in the production of a commodity, if it had not been used in producing that commodity; but could have been used for some other commodity.

The value of one enterprise is sacrificed as a cost in the production of another enterprise. In simple terms, it is the cost equivalent to the returns from the next best alternative foregone.

4) LAW OF FACTOR-SUBSTITUTION

What types of inputs and their combination or production practices should be used, is one of the basic farm management decisions. It involves the factor–factor relationship or the principle of substitution between inputs. This principle provides for the determination of the least cost method of production. It says that if the quantity of output is constant, it is economical to substitute one factor of production for another factor, if the cost of the first is less than that of the second.

The principle of factor substitution says further; go on adding a resource so long as the additional cost of the resource being added is less than the saving in cost from the resource being replaced. Thus if input X_1 is being increased (added) and input X_2 is being replaced, increase the use of X_1, so long as:

Decrease in cost $>$ Increase in cost

(or)

Quantity saved of the replaced   Quantity increased of the
input × price of the replaced input $>$ added input × price of the
                                            added input

(or)

$$\frac{\text{Quantity saved of the replaced input}}{\text{Quantity increased of the added input}} > \frac{\text{Price of the added input}}{\text{Price of the replaced input}}$$

(or)

MRS $>$ Price ratio

i.e. $\dfrac{\Delta X_2}{\Delta X_1}$ $>$ $\dfrac{P_{x_1}}{P_{x_2}}$

Procedure for Working Out the Least Cost Combination

1) Compute the substitution ratio (MRS) by dividing the number of units of the replaced resource by the number of units of the added resource.

$$MRS = \frac{\text{No of units of replaced resource}}{\text{No. of units of added resource}} = \frac{\Delta X_2}{\Delta X_1}$$

2) Compute the price ratio by dividing the price of the added resources by the price of the replaced resource.

$$PR = \frac{\text{Cost per unit of added resource}}{\text{Cost per unit of replaced resource}} = \frac{P_{x_1}}{P_{x_2}}$$

3) Find out the point where the substitution ratio's and price ratio are equal.

$$\frac{\Delta X_2}{\Delta X_1} = \frac{P_{x_1}}{P_{x_2}} \text{ or } \Delta X_1 \cdot P_{x_1} = \Delta X_2 \cdot P_{x_2}$$

Profit Rules

1) If the substitution ratio is greater than the price ratio, one can reduce the costs by using the more of added resources (Δx_1).

2) If the substitution ratio is less than the price ratio, costs can be reduced by using more of replaced resources (Δx_2).

3) If the substitution ratio equals the price ratio it is the point of least cost.

When the resource combination is in fixed proportions (complements), only one combination is possible in production process, which require combination of two resources in fixed proportions. Factors must be combined in the manner dictated by this extreme technique of production. When the factors substitute continuously at constant marginal rates, only one of the two unique combinations will maximise the cost of producing a given output. The given output should be produced entirely with X_1 and none of X_2, if the MRS is less than price ratio. The same level of output can be produced entirely with X_2 and none of X_1, if the MRS is greater than price ratio; when the same cost outlay results from various combinations, any combination of X_1 and X_2 resources can be used.

The principles explained above can be extended to any number of factors. If the production process can employ three substitute resources X_1, X_2, and X_3, minimum costs for a given output are realised when:

$$\frac{\Delta X_1}{\Delta X_2} = \frac{P_{x_2}}{P_{x_1}}, \quad \frac{\Delta X_3}{\Delta X_2} = \frac{P_{x_2}}{P_{x_3}} \text{ and } \frac{\Delta X_3}{\Delta X_1} = \frac{P_{x_1}}{P_{x_3}}$$

For combination of more than two inputs, the same principle can be extended.

a) When marginal physical products (MPP) and price of the inputs are considered:

$$\frac{MPP_{x_1}}{P_{x_1}} = \frac{MPP_{x_2}}{P_{x_2}} = \frac{MPP_{x_3}}{P_{x_3}} = \cdots = \frac{MPP_{x_n}}{P_{x_n}}.$$

b) When marginal value products (MVP) and the prices of inputs are concerned:

$$\frac{MVP_{x_1}}{P_{x_1}} = \frac{MVP_{x_2}}{P_{x_2}} = \frac{MVP_{x_3}}{P_{x_3}} = \cdots = \frac{MVP_{x_n}}{P_{x_n}} = 1.$$

Here the MVP's are equal to the prices of the concerned inputs.

5) Principle of Product Substitution

The suitability of more than one enterprise on the farm poses an important management question to the farmer: What combination of different enterprises would yield maximum profit? The problem is to determine a suitable combination of products for a given outlay of resources.

The principle of product substitution, complementary, and supplementary relationships, the law of equimarginal returns and the opportunity cost principle are used in deciding the optimal combination of enterprises. The product-production relationships, the possibilities of competitive relationship is the most common between enterprises. When the enterprises are competitive, three things determine the exact combination of the products which would be most profitable:

a) The rate at which one enterprise substitute for the others.

b) The prices of the products.

c) The cost of producing the competing products.

If the cost of production of the two enterprises is the same, the farmer will be guided by the first two factors, i.e. MRS and prices of products. Substitute one enterprise for the other, so long as the net income gained is more than the net income sacrificed.

In case the cost of production of two enterprises is different, it is adjusted to the prices of the products.

The unit cost of production of each enterprise is deducted from its price, which is then used to compute the price ratio (net price ratio). The rule says, so long as MRS is less than the inverse of price ratio of the products, it pays to increase the enterprise being added·

$$\frac{\Delta Y_2}{\Delta Y_1} < \frac{P_{y_1}}{P_{y_2}} \quad \text{increase } Y_1 \text{ production.}$$

$$\frac{\Delta Y_2}{\Delta Y_1} = \frac{P_{y_1}}{P_{y_2}} \quad \text{is the point of maximum profits.}$$

Table 5.6. Constant rate of product substitution and profit
maximisation

Production possibilities		MRS of Y_2 for Y_1 $\Delta Y_1/\Delta Y_2$	Revenue under three price situations		
Y_1	Y_2		P_{y_1}= Rs. 2.50 P_{y_2}= Rs. 2.50	P_{y_1} = Rs. 4 P_{y_2} = Rs. 5	P_{y_1}= Rs. ? P_{y_2}= Rs. 10
80	0		200	320	400
72	4	2	202	308	400
64	8	2	204	296	400
56	12	2	206	284	400
48	16	2	208	272	400
40	20	2	210	260	400
32	24	2	212	248	400
24	28	2	214	236	400
16	32	2	216	224	400
8	36	2	218	212	400
0	40	2	220	200	400

Table 5.7. Increasing rates of substitution and profit maximisation

Production possibilities		MRS of $\Delta Y_1/\Delta Y_2$	Revenue under two price situations	
Y_1	Y_2		P_{y_1} = Rs. 2.00 P_{y_2} = Rs. 4.00	P_{y_1} = Rs. 2.00 P_{y_2}= Rs. 8.00
265	0	1.4	530	530
251	10	1.8	542	582
233	20	2.2	546	626
211	30	2.6	542	662
185	40	3.0	530	690
155	50	3.4	510	710
121	60	3.8	482	722
83	70	4.0	446	726
43	80	4.3	406	726
0	90		360	720

Table 5.6 gives the production possibility schedule under constant rate
of substitution for 20 units of resources. Under first price situation, the
marginal rate of substitution i.e. 2 is less than the price ratio. In this
situation, profits can be increased by substituting Y_2 for Y_1 continuously.

Under the second price situation, the substitution ratio $\dfrac{(\Delta Y_1)}{(\Delta Y_2)} = 2.0$ is

Table 5.8. Decreasing rate of substitution and profit maximisation

Production possibilities		MRS of $\Delta Y_1/\Delta Y_2$	Revenue under two price situations (Rs)	
Y_1	Y_2		P_{y_1} = Rs. 5 P_{y_2} = Rs. 10	P_{y_1} = Rs. 5 P_{y_2} = Rs. 5
40.00	0	– 1.20	400.00	200.00
34.00	5	– 1.10	365.00	195.00
28.50	10	– 1.00	335.00	192.50
23.50	15	– 0.90	310.00	192.50
19.00	20	– 0.80	290.00	195.00
15.00	25	– 0.70	275.00	200.00
11.50	30	– 0.60	265.00	207.50
8.50	35	– 0.50	260.00	217.50
6.00	40	– 0.40	260.00	230.00
4.00	45	– 0.35	265.00	245.00
2.25	50	– 0.25	272.50	261.25
1.00	55	– 0.20	285.00	280.00
0	60		300.00	300.00

greater than the price ratio of $\frac{4}{5}$ and profits can be increased by substituting Y_1 for Y_2 rather than Y_2 for Y_1. Therefore, the producer should specialise in one or the other of the two products under constant rates of substitution, if the price and substitution ratios are not equal. Under price situation three, when the price and substitution ratios are equal, the producer can take up any of the several combinations. All the combinations will bring the same revenue.

When two products Y_1 and Y_2 substitute at increasing rates, the production possibilities are indicated in Table 5.7. Increasing amounts of Y_1 are sacrificed or replaced for each unit increase in Y_2 and vice versa. In the first price situation, the price ratio $\frac{4}{2} = 2.0$ is equal to the substitution ratio between 233 and 211 units of Y_1, 20 and 30 units of Y_2. Between these ranges, the profits are maximum at Rs. 546. Under second price situation, the price ratio is $\frac{8}{2} = 4.00$ which is equal to substitution ratio $\frac{Y_1}{Y_2}$ at 43 units of Y_1 and 80 units of Y_2 and the total revenue is also maximum at Rs.726. The price ratio falling in the range of 1.4 and 4.3 will lead to some output combinations of both Y_1 and Y_2 products, while price ratio falling outside this range must lead to specialisation of one product, either Y_1 or Y_2.

The production possibility schedule for decreasing rates of product substitution was presented in Table 5.8. Under the first price situation, the price ratio was $\frac{10}{5} = 2$, revenue can be at a maximum with the production of Y_2 alone. When the price ratio is $\frac{5}{5} = 1$, by specialising in Y_1 production, this will bring the substitution ratio less than price ratio. Diversification is never profitable when two products are produced under conditions of increasing returns.

When the competitive products substituted at constant rates and their price and substitution ratio's are not equal, the producer should specialise in one or the other of the two products. Thus only one of the two pattern of resource use define maximum profits. When the ratios are equal, the producers can be indifferent and any one of the several combinations will bring the same revenue. When the products substitute at increasing rates, which is a common relationship in agriculture, diversification will predominate. When products substitute at decreasing rate, the tendency is towards specialisation.

6) PRINCIPLE OF COMPARATIVE ADVANTAGES

According to this well known principle, different areas will tend to produce those products for which they have the greatest comparative and not just absolute advantage. This leads to the establishment of different types of farming existing in a particular area. The main factors involved in the law are simply an extension and application of principles of specialisation and diversification. The physical and economic conditions influence the production from region to region, farm to farm and even within a farm from field to field.

There are two types of advantages in raising the farm produce on the basis of maximum net revenue per hectare.

a) Absolute advantage
b) Relative advantage

a) Absolute advantage—Net return/hectare

Crop: Paddy	Region-A	Region-B
Total income	500.00	375.00
Total expenditure	425.00	350.00
Net return/ha	75.00	25.00
Return/rupee	1.18	1.07
Return is greater than cost by	118%	107%

Crop: Sugarcane		
Total income	1,000.00	1,500.00
Total expenditure	475.00	500.00
Net return/ha	525.00	1,000.00
Return/rupee	2.10	3.00
Return is greater than cost by	210%	300%

From the above figures, it will be seen that region-A has an absolute advantage in paddy, because the net income per hectare or per rupee spent is greater than that of region-B. Region-B has an absolute advantage in sugarcane, because the income from sugarcane is 300% greater than the cost.

Region-A has a greater absolute advantage in growing both paddy and groundnut than C, because the net income per hectare are Rs. 75.00 and Rs.25.00, respectively. In otherwords respective incomes are 118% and 113% higher than costs. Farmers of region-A can make profit by growing both the crops. But they want to make the greater profit, which can be done by having the largest possible acreage under paddy alone, as it is a question of relative advantage.

b, Relative or comparative advantage

	Region A	Region C	
	Groundnut	Groundnut	Paddy
Total income/ha	225.00	220.00	225.00
Total expenditure/ha	200.00	200.00	210.00
Net income/ha	25.00	20.00	15.00
Return per rupee spent	1.13	1.16	1.07
Per cent return above cost of input	113%	116%	107%

Similarly, farmers of the region-C can make some profit by growing paddy, but they have relative advantage in growing groundnut. They make greater profit by growing groundnut, the percentage return over the cost of production being 107% for paddy and 116% for groundnut.

How Does the Law Direct the Farmer in Farming?

The law of comparative advantage directs a farmer in the selection of those crop and livestock enterprises, in the production of which available resources have the great relative and not absolute advantage. Thus, fruit and vegetable farming near the cities, sugarcane farming around the sugar-factories, paddy farming in the low-lying humid region and sheep farming in the hills are outcome of the operation of this principle. The specialised or diversified farming depends largely on the principle of comparative advantage.

7) *Time Comparison Principle*

In deciding about the fixed investment which is made either in one lumpsum such as buying a tractor, constructing a building, investment in a tube-well, etc., or in stages such as orchard growing, where the outcome or the resultant income is a flow of incomes after a certain interval, the effect of time has to be considered. In such situations, the principle of time comparison is applied. Such time adjustments relate to taking account of:

1) Time element in the calculation of present value of future incomes.

2) The risks and uncertainties involved in farm operations over time.

These adjustments involve a method of discounting future returns and compounding costs. In other words, this would enable the present worth of a future decision and decide whether it is worth while at all in effecting changes in crop production or effecting an improvement in farming business.

Two aspects of the problem are considered under such situations:

i) Growth of a cash investment over time.

ii). Discounting of future income.

The cash investment grows over time due to the compounding of interest charges of opportunity costs involved in using the capital. The formula used in calculating the growth of cash investment is that of compound interest rate, which is:

$$A = P\left(1 + \frac{r}{100}\right)^n$$

A = investment at the end of n periods;

P = initial amount which is invested for n periods;

r = rate of interest; and n = number of years.

Discounting income is the procedure, whereby the present value of the future income is determined. The concept is the reverse of 'growth in value'.

$$P = \frac{A}{\left(1 + \frac{r}{100}\right)^n} \quad \text{i.e.} \quad Pv = \frac{I}{\left(1 + \frac{r}{100}\right)^n}$$

Pv is present value of the future expected incomes, or returns $A(I)$

Thus with interest at the rate of 10%, Rs. 100 today grows to Rs. 110

in a year and conversely Rs. 110 a year from now is worth only Rs. 100 at present, when discounted at 10%.

If we lend money to some one to use, we can normally expect to be paid interest for the use of that money. In the same manner, banks will pay interest on deposits. If we lend money to some one else means, we are differing our use of present money for future. If we do this, we are entitled to be rewarded and interest is that reward for waiting. If a farmer lends money to his neighbour, the farmer is passing on the opportunity to use the money for a productive purpose. It is then reasonable that the lender be compensated for the income foregone and the borrower pays something for the use of lenders money. Thus interest is related to current income foregone.

With a view to ascertaining the profitability of an investment, benefits which are spread over the entire life of the investment, activity cannot be added and compared with the capital expenditure incurred at one point of time, because these two items are uncomparable.

The rate of growth of a cash outlay over time depends primarily on the interest rate. Since costs grow as a result of interest or opportunity cost accumulations, the equations for compounding interest, which is given above can be put as:

$$S = S_1 (1 + r)^n.$$

S represents the sum at the end of n periods; S_1 represents the amount which is invested for n periods and r is the interest rate. If the interest has to be compounded semi-annually, the annual interest rate would have to be divided by two and n multiplied by two. Likewise, if the costs are to be compounded m times, the r should be divided by m and n multiplied by m.

The above equation is appropriate when resource services are given off in their entirety at the end of a given number of periods. However, in most cases capital investments gradually depreciate.

The appropriate equation to use in such cases is:

$$S = S_1 (1 + r) + S_2 (1 + r)^2 + S_3 (1 + r)^3 + ... + S_n (1 + r)^n.$$

where S_1, S_2, S_3 and S_n refer to the amount of the initial investment given off at the end of the first, second, third and nth years.

Example 1: An example is given in Table 5.9.

Discounting Techniques: (Present Worth Factor): The present value of a given income in a future year is derived by using the equation:

$$PV = \frac{I}{(1 + r)^n}$$

Table 5.9. Annual investments and returns and their compound costs
of coconut plantation for five-year period

Year	Investment Rs.	Compounded investment @ 10% annual interest Rs.	Returns Rs.	Compounded returns @ 10% annual interest Rs.
1st	6,500	10,468.25	-	-
2nd	7,000	10,248.70	-	-
3rd	5,200	6,921.20	-	-
4th	5,000	6,050.00	9,000	9,900
5th	3,500	3,815.00	20,000	24,200
Total	27,200	37,503.75	29,000	34,100

PV = Present value; I is the future income, r is the discount rate, n is the number of years before the income will be received. This is the equation to use, when future income is discounted on an annual basis. If the income is discounted m times per year (half-yearly, quarterly, etc.) i should be divided by m and n multiplied by m. An example is given in Table 5.10.

The present value of a sequence of annual incomes is given by the equation:

$$V = \frac{I_1}{(1+r)} + \frac{I_2}{(1+r)^2} + \frac{I_3}{(1+r)^3} + \cdots + \frac{I_n}{(1+r)^n}$$

I represents annual income, which may or may not be the same each year. This equation is used to compute present value. However, when income is constant and continues in perpetuity, the above equation is reduced to

$$V = \frac{I}{r}.$$

Example 2:

Type of investment	=	Agricultural machinery
Estimated economic life	=	3 years
Cost of investment	=	Rs. 1,000
Rate of interest	=	10% per annum

Annual benefits:

Year		Amount (Rs.)
1	=	200
2	=	400
3	=	600
Total	=	1,200

Table 5.10. Present value of future benefits from investment

Year	Investment Cost Rs.	Compounded cost @ 10% R.I. (Rs.)	Benefits (Rs.)	Present value of benefits Rs.
1	1,000		200	182
2	—		400	330
3	—		600	451
Total	1,000	1,464.10	1,200	963

PRODUCTION FUNCTIONS

The most popular production functions used in farm resource management and decision making process are presented with relevant examples.

1) Linear Function

The simplest form of linear production function is $Y = a_0 + bx$, with one variable input and $Y = a_0 + b_1 x_1 + b_2 x_2 + b_3 x_3 + ... + b_n x_n$ with n variables, where Y = output, X_i = inputs, a_0 = constant. In fitting a simple linear production function, the following six basic quantities must be obtained.

$$n, \bar{x}, \bar{y}, \Sigma x^2, \Sigma y^2 \text{ and } \Sigma xy$$

n = Number of observations

$\bar{x}$ and $\bar{y}$ = Mean values of x and y

$$\Sigma x^2 = \Sigma x^2 - \frac{(\Sigma x)^2}{n}$$

$$\Sigma y^2 = \Sigma y^2 - \frac{(\Sigma y)^2}{n}$$

$$\Sigma xy = \Sigma xy - \frac{(\Sigma x)(\Sigma y)}{n}$$

$b = \dfrac{\Sigma xy}{\Sigma x^2}$, b = regression coefficient

$a_0 = \bar{Y} + b(x - \bar{x})$, a_0 = constant

Example

$$Y = b_0 x_0 + b_1 x_1 + b_2 x_2 + b_3 x_3 + b_4 x_4 + b_5 x_5$$

where Y = income

l_i = unknown parameters to be estimated

x_1 = expenditure on improved seeds

x_2 = expenditure on fertilisers
x_3 = expenditure on plant protection
x_4 = irrigation charges
x_5 = cropped area per farm

The estimated equation is:

$$Y = 0.2151 + 0.0412\, x_1 - 0.0002\, x_2 + 0.0752\, x_3$$
$$-0.0066\, x_4 - 0.0880\, x_5;$$
$$R^2 = 0.64;\ F \text{ Value} = 3.56.$$

The values of x_i's indicate the rate of change Y due to change in x_i's by one unit. For example, an unit change in x_1 results in 0.0412 units increase in Y, and an unit change in x_2 results in 0.0002 units decrease in Y.

2) Cobb-Douglas Production Function (or) Power Function

General form with one variable is

$$Y = ax^b \tag{1}$$

where Y = output,
  a = constant,
  b = transformation ratio when x is at different magnitudes,
  x = variable resources.

The exponent or b coefficient is the elasticity of production, and can be used directly. This equation estimated in logarithmic form is given by

$$\log Y = \log a + b \log x.$$

General form with n variable resources

When parameters are to be estimated for more than one variable resource, the same algebraic restraints exist for n variables. The power function below has the same characteristics as that of $Y = ax^b$.

$$Y = ax_1^{b_1} x_2^{b_2} \ldots x_n^{b_n}. \tag{2}$$

The regression coefficients b_1 and b_2 derived with the observations in logarithms are the production elasticities of individual resources. Their sum indicate the returns to scale. In log form, the equation is expressed as

$$\log Y = \log a + b_1 \log x_1 + b_2 \log x_2 + \ldots + b_n \log x_n.$$

This function allows either constant, increasing or decreasing marginal productivity. It does not allow an input–output curve embracing all the three. With all other inputs held in fixed magnitude, the marginal product is expected to decline. The marginal product equation is:

$$\frac{dy}{dx} = b \, ax^{\,b-1} = \frac{b \, ax^{\,b}}{x} \qquad (3)$$

indicating that if $b = 1$, the marginal product (also average product) will be constant at the level a, where $b > 1$ the magnitude of marginal product will increase as x increases, depending upon the magnitude of b. If $b = 2$ for example, the marginal products are ba, $2ba$, $3ba$, and $4ba$ when x has the respective values 1, 2, 3, 4. Where $b = 1$, the magnitude of marginal products will decline as x increases, since $x^b < x$.

This function assumes a constant elasticity of production (Ep), over the entire input–output curve, i.e.

$$\frac{dy_1}{dx_1} \cdot \frac{x_1}{y_1} = \frac{dy_2}{dx_2} \cdot \frac{x_2}{y_2} = \cdots = \frac{dy_n}{dx_n} \cdot \frac{x_n}{y_n} \qquad (4)$$

This condition of the equation, that successive equal increments of input add the same percentage to total output, can be proved by multiplying the derivative or marginal product equation [Eq. (3)], by the inverse of the average product (the definition of production elasticity), as shown below:

$$Ep = (b \, ax^{\,b-1}) \frac{x}{y} = \frac{b \, ax^{\,b}}{x} \cdot \frac{x}{y} \qquad (5)$$

Now, substituting the value of Y of Eq. (1) into Eq. (5), we obtain Eq. (6).

$$Ep = \frac{b \, ax^{\,b}}{x} \cdot \frac{x}{y} = \frac{b \, y}{x} \cdot \frac{x}{y} \qquad (6)$$

or $Ep = b$.

Since Y's and X's cancel, we have $Ep = b$, or the elasticity is a constant equal to the exponent of x in Eq. (1).

The power function $Y = ax_1^{b_1} x_2^{b_2} \cdots x_n^{b_n}$ has the same mathematical characteristics as in the equation $Y = ax^b$ for n resources, when input–output curves are derived for one resource with the other held constant. The assumptions of constant elasticity and marginal products with only a plus or minus sign, regardless of input or output magnitude are retained.

The regression coefficients $b_1, b_2, \dots, b_n$ derived with observations in logarithms are the production elasticities of the individual resources. Their sum indicates the nature of *returns to scale*, provided $x_1 x_2 \cdots x_n$ are the only relevant resource.

1) With the sum $b_1 + b_2 + ... + b_n = 1$, a given percentage increase in n inputs, will result in an equal percentage in output.

2) With elasticity sums being more or less than one, output will increase by a greater or smaller percentage, respectively, than inputs.

Example 3

Let Y =   Gross income in rupees per hectare

x_1 =   Land in hectares

x_2 =   Machine labour in hours

x_3 =   Irrigation charges in rupees

x_4 =   Human labour in rupees

x_5 =   Seed in kgs.

x_6 =   Plant protection measures in rupees

x_7 =   Fertilisers in rupees.

After fitting the multiple regression formula to the above variables in logarithmic form, wherein the information on the variables are collected from 150 sampled farms, the final result of the Cobb-Douglas Production Function is as follows:

$$Log Y = 0.7342 + 0.63\overset{..}{1}5\, x_1 + 0.0234\, x_2 - 0.0496\, x_3 + 0.19\overset{..}{0}4\, x_4$$

$$+ 0.07\overset{..}{6}0\, x_5 - 0.0286\, x_6 + 0.0871\, x_7$$

or

$$Y = 0.7342\, x_1^{0.6315} x_2^{0.0234} x_3^{-0.0496} x_4^{0.1904} x_5^{0.0760}$$

$$x_6^{-0.0285} x_7^{0.0871}$$

The values above are simply the regression coefficients of log Y on log x_1, log x_2, ..., log x_7 or simply the elasticities of production with respect to these resource inputs, and the asterik (*) indicates their statistical significance at 5% probability levels, respectively. They tell the percentage increase in Y with one per cent increase in input x. For example, if we increase x_1 by one per cent, holding other resources at a constant level, Y will increase by 0.6315 per cent, thus showing diminishing return with respect to land input. Diminishing factor returns were observed for land, human labour, seed. For irrigation and plant protection measures, the factor returns were negative and significant, which indicate excessive use of these resources. The sum of elasticities turn out to be less than un (0.9308), which revealed diminishing scale returns.

The marginal value productivities of factors taken at their prevailing

---

** indicate significance at 10 per cent probability level

market prices or opportunity costs indicate the efficiency of resour᷂.
MVPs that are higher than opportunity or market costs of factors, in a
cate the scope of raising output profitably through the increased use of
resources concerned, whereas those less than the opportunity or market
costs, depict unprofitable nature of resource use. Any factor is considered to be used most efficiently, if its MVP is just sufficient to offset
its cost. Equality of MVP to factor cost is therefore the basic condition,
that should be satisfied to find out the efficient use of resources.

The MVPs from the power function can be estimated by the following
formula:

$$\text{MVP of } x_i = b_i \frac{\bar{Y}}{\bar{X}_i}$$

Where $\bar{Y}$ = geometric mean of yield,

x_i = geometric mean of ith independent variable and

b_i = the regression coefficient of the ith independent variable.

The MVP to opportunity cost ratio of land and fertilisers was more than
one, suggesting more profits can be obtained with the increase in these
resources. The ratio's for other resources turned out to be less than their
market prices/opportunity costs revealing inefficient use of these resources (Table 5.11).

Table 5.11. Marginal value productivities and opportunity costs and
resource use efficiency on rice farms in Andhra Pradesh

Varia-bles	Sample means	MVPs	Opportunity costs (Rs.)	MVP to opportunity cost ratio's
Y	16.4586	—	—	—
x_1	0.9790	2,231.3470	1,060.13	2.10
x_2	3.7489	21.5685	32.55	0.66
x_3	53.6414	-3.1978	0.78	-4.10
x_4	1,265.0276	0.5219	0.69	0.76
x_5	369.9985	0.7117	1.00	0.71
x_6	67.9360	-1.4518	1.00	-1.45
x_7	92.0874	3.2737	1.00	3.27

3) Quadratic Form

The quadratic equation $Y = a + bx - cx^2$, with a minus before C
denotes diminishing marginal returns, does not impose such strict restric-
tions on the production function, as does the Cobb-Douglas equation. It
allows both a declining and negative marginal productivity, but not both

increasing and decreasing marginal products. A maximum total product is defined where input magnitude or x is equal to $0.5\ bc^{-1}$. The elasticity is not constant, as in the power function, but declines with input magnitude as indicated by the elasticity equation.

$$Ep = \frac{bx - 2cx^2}{a + bx - cx^2} \qquad (7)$$

As indicated by equation $\dfrac{dy}{dx} = b - 2cx$

use of the quadratic equation does assume a particular characteristic in relationship between marginal products, namely they decline by a constant absolute amount, or

$m_i = m_{i-1}\ K$, where
m_i = marginal product of ith input
m_{i-1} = marginal product of the $(i-1)$th input
K = constant, by which successive marginal products decline; $K = 2C$

Increasing Marginal Productivity

A production function embracing both increasing and decreasing marginal productivity is seldom needed for a single variable resource where needed, a function allowing this condition is the polynomial

$$Y = a + bx + cx^2 - dx^3 \qquad (8)$$

It has increasing marginal products, until x is equal to $0.3333\ cd^{-1}$, than diminishing but positive marginal products until

$$x = 0.3333\ d^{-1}c + (3db + c^2)^{0.5}$$

which is the value of x that maximises total product. Supposing a to be zero, the elasticity is, (1) greater than one (stage-1) for $0 < x < 0.5\ cd^{-1}$, (2) equal to one (constant returns) at $x = 0.5\ cd^{-1}$ and (3) less than one but greater than zero for $x \geq 0.5\ cd^{-1}$ (stage-2). Marginal products decrease at an increasing rate in the latter stage.

Extension of the quadratic form in equation $Y = a + bx - cx^2$, to two or more resources results in the production surface equation as:

$$Y = a + b_1 x_1 + b_2 x_2 - b_3 x_1^2 - b_4 x_2^2 + b_5 x_1 x_2 \qquad (9)$$

Diminishing marginal returns exist for either factor alone, but there is positive interaction between the two factors. Negative or zero interaction also may exist, where diminishing marginal returns hold true for both factors. The equation might be presented with only positive signs for the b_i's. However, it is logical that the signs are negative for b_3 and b_4 and either positive or negative for b_5. Yet the general algebraic relationships are the same regardless of the signs used.

USE OF QUADRATIC PRODUCTION FUNCTION IN ESTIMATING PROFIT MAXIMISING QUANTITIES OF INPUTS

Profit is maximised for the fixed unit, if the marginal value product of the factor is equal to the marginal cost of the factor

$$Y = a + bx - cx^2 \qquad (10)$$

Y = magnitude of output,

x = magnitude of input, and

b & c = positive constants.

The total value product v is given by Eq. (11), where output in Eq. (10) is multiplied by P_y, the price of the product

$$V = P_y Y = aP_y + bP_y x - cP_y x^2 \qquad (11)$$

The MVP is the derivative of Eq. (11), while the marginal cost if Px, the price of the resource in a competitive market. Equating the marginal value product of the resource with its marginal cost, we obtain Eq. (12).

$$\frac{dv}{dx} = bP_y - 2cP_y \ x = P_x \qquad (12)$$

Transposing the terms of dividing by the coefficient of x, we specify the magnitude of input, which will maximise profit as that in Eq. (13) below:

$$bP_y - 2cP_y x = P_x$$
$$bP_y - 2cP_y x - P_x = 0$$
$$bP_y - P_x = 2cP_y x$$

$$\frac{bP_y - P_x}{2c \, P_y} = X \qquad (13)$$

The coefficients b and c will ordinarily be derived from regression equations estimated from experimental or sample data. With these estimates available and knowing the product and factor prices as P_y and P_x these quantities can be substituted into Eq. 4. With the magnitude of x specified accordingly, the value of x indicates the magnitude of input or experiment treatment, which will maximise profit from the fixed factor. The optimum quantity of input is a function of factor and product price with b and c being constants in the production function. As P_x increases, the optimum magnitude of x declines. As P_y increases, the optimum level of x increases. A decline in factor and product prices will have opposite effect on the optimum magnitude of x.

Profit from the use of factor also is maximised when its marginal product is equated to the price ratio

$$\frac{d_y}{d_x} = \frac{P_x}{P_y}.$$

The marginal product of the factor is the first derivative of the production function. $Y = a + bx - cx^2$. Setting the derivative of this equation to equal to the factor of product-price ratio, we obtain Eq. 14.

$$b - 2cx = \frac{P_x}{P_y} \tag{14}$$

Transposing and dividing by $2c$, we obtain the quantity of x, which maximises profit, it is again that determined by Eq. (13), i.e.,

$$\frac{bP_y - P_x}{2cP_y} = x.$$

From Eq. (14) it is obvious that to maximise profit, the marginal product will need to decrease through the addition of X, as factor price decreases relative to product price. An increase in the magnitude of P_x relative to P_y will call for an increase in magnitude of the marginal product $b - 2cx$ by a reduction in magnitude of x.

Example 4:

The Agricultural Research Station, Maruteru, Andhra Pradesh conducted a varietal and fertiliser response trials for rice, var. Vasistha. The response equation fitted is $Y = a + bx - cx^2$, a quadratic form of function, wherein

Y = yield/ha in kg,
a = constant,
b and c = regression coefficients indicating transformation ratios of different orders of magnitudes of x, and
x = nitrogen applied / ha in kg.

The response equation obtained from the experimental data is:

$$Y = 4437 + 23.71x - 0.26x^2$$
$$\frac{dy}{dx} = b - 2cx = \frac{P_x}{P_y}$$
$$= 23.71 - 2(0.26x) = \frac{4.02}{0.82}$$

$$= 23.71 - 0.52x = \frac{4.02}{0.82}$$

$(b - 2cx) P_y = (23.71 - 0.52x) 0.84 = 4.02 = P_x$

$bP_y - 2cxP_y = 19.9164 - 0.4368x = 4.02$

$bP_y - P_x = 2cxP_y = 19.9164 - 4.02 = 0.4368x$

$$= 15.8964 = 0.4368x$$

$$\frac{bP_y - P_x}{2cP_y} = x = \frac{15.8964}{0.4368} = 36\cdot3928$$

The quantity of x (nitrogen) which maximises profit is 36.39 kg of nitrogen, when P_y = Rs. 0.84/kg and P_x is Rs. 4.02/kg.

CHAPTER 6
Farm Resource Management

LAND MANAGEMENT

SELECTION OF FARM

Choice of farm arises when there is sufficient culturable land for use or there is no restriction for sanction of purchase of land.

FACTORS TO BE CONSIDERED IN SELECTING A FARM

1) Physical Factors
   a) Climate
   b) Rainfall
   c) Topography
   d) Soil
   e) Water supply
   f) Drainage

2) Economic Factors
   a) Transport and market facilities
   b) Institutional facilities like co-operatives, land, etc.
   c) Local taxes
   d) Land values and productivity

3) Social Factors
   a) Accessibility to school and hospitals
   b) Type of neighbours and community
   c) Tradition and customs

SIZE OF FARM

The size of farm is generally understood in terms of physical area, volume of production and value of production.

In general the size of farm refers to physical area, but in terms of economics this refers to either with the volume of production or value of production.

Minimum Efficient Size

The minimum size of a farm should be such as will keep the farmer fully employed and will just provide him with an income sufficient to sustain himself and his family.

Economic Size of a Farm

The family farm is one in which all the factors of production would be wholly within the family farm. Hence the economic size of the farm should be somewhat larger than the minimum efficient and should provide a reasonable standard of living to the family.

It could also be stated that the economic size of a farm should allow a man the chance of producing sufficient to support himself and his family in a reasonable comfort after paying his necessary expenses.

It is not easy to determine the economic size of the farm for the country as a whole. It will vary from place to place. It should be studied in relation to specific region, in terms of the fertility and location of the farms, irrigation facilities, nature of crops grown, amount of capital available for investment and managerial capacity of the farmers.

Factors Effecting the Size of Farms

1) Financial resources
2) Density of population
3) Climate
4) Topography
5) Nature and source of irrigation
6) Nature of crops grown
7) Nature of cultivation
8) Managerial capacity
9) Law of inheritance
10) State laws

ACQUIRING AND APPRAISING THE VALUE OF A FARM

In acquiring a farm, the following factors are to be considered.
1) Farm layout
2) Cropping pattern and cropping scheme that is possible
3) Physical factors
4) Economic factors
5) Personal likes and dislikes

1) Farm Layout

Layout of a farm refers to the manner in which the farm is divided into fields and the location and arrangement of other fixtures, such as irrigation and drainage system, building and sheds, etc. The layout of a farm directly affects:

a) Costs and efficiency in the use of manpower, bullock power and machinery.

b) Costs and efficiency of irrigation, drainage, fencing, etc.

c) Cropping plan and profitability of the farm business as a whole.

2) Cropping Pattern

Cropping pattern refers to adoption of a particular type of crops by the farmers in a particular region. It is expressed at a macro level, i.e. district, taluk or village level.

3) Cropping System

Refers to the sequence of crops grown to maintain the fertility status of the soil.

4) Factors Influencing Cropping Pattern

1) Climatic factors
2) Intensity of population and labour availability
3) Consumption habits and socio-economic factors of the people in a region
4) Institutional set-up
5) Transport, communication, storage and market facilities

5) Cropping Scheme

The plan according to which crops are raised on individual plots of a farm with the object of getting maximum returns from each crop and without impairing soil fertility is called cropping scheme. This refers to micro level. To increase returns from a given area of land, multiple cropping, relay cropping, intercropping and mixed cropping can be followed in the cropping scheme.

Appraising the Value of Farm (Methods of Estimating the Value of Land)

There are three methods for the determination of the values of land.

1) Income capitalisation method
2) Comparison method
3) Sale price method

1) INCOME CAPITALISATION METHOD

The value of land and any other asset on its current income in relation to the prevailing rate of interest is called capitalized value. The use of income capitalisation method requires the following factors.

Normal Appraisal Method

Generally, for quick economic decision the value of land is determined by capitalising the expected net income by the expected rate of interest on long-term investment.

Example 1: Annual net income = Gross income from crops minus
                    total cost
Rate of interest is a capitalisation rate.

When income is constant, the formula used is: $V = \dfrac{I}{r}$

V = Capitalised value of land

I = Net income or return per year

r = Rate of interest

When income rise or fall at a constant arithmatic rate

$$V = \frac{I}{r} \pm \frac{I}{r^2}$$

where I is increase or decrease in net income per year.

The value of land under Indian conditions may be determined by adopting either of the following criteria:

1) Multiple of the value of gross produce of land.
2) Multiple of the value of net produce or income of land.
3) Sale value of land.
4) Capitalising the rent of land.

Each of the above criteria may prove useful in particular circumstances.

The Capitalisation Method

The capitalisation method of appraisal is based largely upon the capacity of a farm to produce net income. In using this method, it usually is assumed that the values of farms in an area will have a fairly consistent relation to the average annual net incomes they will produce over a period of years. The relation or ratio, which farm values in an area may have to net incomes is called the capitalisation rate for the area. Comparisons between actual net incomes and values in the area will give one measure of the capitalisation rate to use.

The capitalisation method may be illustrated by listing some summary data for a hypothetical farm. First the appraiser sets up a cropping pattern

and livestock programme, likely to be followed by a typical operator on
the farm in the future. He then estimates the amount of average annual
gross income that will be received from sales of crops and livestock to
be Rs. 15,000. Taxes and depreciation on buildings and equipment are
estimated at Rs. 1200 per year. Farm production expenses total to
Rs. 4500 and operator and family labour and management are valued at
Rs. 3500. The appraiser summarises these estimates as follows:

Gross farm income = Rs. 15,000
Deductions:
Taxes & depreciation = Rs. 1,200
Production expenses = Rs. 4,500
Value of labour and management = Rs. 3,500

Total deductions = Rs. 9,200

Net remaining to land and buildings = Rs. 4 800

Now, when the net income is capitalised at 10 per cent, the estimate
of value of the farm is given by:

$$V = \frac{I}{r}$$, where I is the net income, r is the capitalisation rate
(interest rate).

Therefore, the capitalised value of the farm is

$$\frac{4800}{10} \times 100 = Rs.\ 48,000.$$

In most cases, an appraiser will make certain adjustments in the value
obtained from the capitalisation method. He may increase the value
somewhat, if the farm has several desirable attributes. Factors which
might add to the value would include proximity to market, an efficient
farm layout, good general condition, suitable drainage and absence of
soil erosion. But the appraiser might discount the capitalisation value, if
he should see some risks or weaknesses.

2) Comparative Method of Appraisal

This method attempts to take the best parts of the other two appraisal
methods and combine them into a unified approach. Three general steps
must be taken to place this method into operation.

a) Policy Determination

The appraiser first takes a broad look at long term trends in farm product prices, farm costs and farm real estate values. Past trends are examined and probable future levels are considered. Any unusual factors that may have affected recent trends and relationships will be discounted.

b) *Values for Bench Mark Farms*

Policy determinations made under (a) are then applied in the appraisal of carefully selected and representative bench mark, or key farms in each area. Values for these key farms are carefully estimated by comparisons with actual sales of similar farms. It is then determined whether the net income based on the policy assumptions, represents a reasonable rate of return on that amount of investment. This method of appraisal differs from the capitalisation method, in that the rate of return is used as a check on appraised value rather than allowing a predetermined rate of return to be a determining factor.

c) *Appraising the Individual Farm*

When the appraiser appraises an individual farm, he uses the same general standards in estimating income, as were applied to the bench mark farms in the area. The farm being appraised is related to the most comparable bench mark farm, with respect to income and value characteristics.

Many authorities consider the comparative approach as the most scientific and soundly based method being used in appraising farm real estates, because essentially it is a combination of several approaches and gives the most dependable estimate of the value of farm.

3) The Sale Price Method of Appraisal

This method attempts to estimate the value of a farm as closely as possible to the price that would be paid for it by a typical buyer. To do this, the appraiser usually assembles information on farms in the area have been sold, in past years. He then uses these actual sales data to estimate a reasonable market value for the farm being appraised.

Appraisals based on sales prices have an advantage, in that they can closely approximate true market values. Sometimes the sales price method has a distinct disadvantage of over pricing of the farm. This may be from the optimism generated by a temporary boom in the demand for land.

The following example illustrates the determination of the value of land. In this case the government acquired the agricultural land of some farmers for the purpose of public utility. For the purpose of paying the compensation to the farmers, the land acquisition authorities in Andhra Pradesh had followed the following procedure. There are no trees, wells or other structures in the land under acquisition and is situated by the side of Railway track. For the purpose of determination of the value of lands, the rates that obtained during the period of three years preceding the date of publication of the demand notice of acquisition, the sale statistics have been obtained.

According to the statement of sale statistics furnished by the Mandal Revenue Officer in the area, there are five sales in the vicinity of lands under acquisition during the crucial period. They are as follows (Table 6.1):

Table 6.1. Sale statistics

Sl. No.	Survey Number (S.No.)	Extent sold (acres)	Amount of sale	Rate per acre (0.40 ha)	Dates of sales
			Rs.	Rs.	
1	364/2	0.55	8,800	16,000	20.12.85
2	364/3	0.12	3,000	25,000	14.2.86
3	364/3	0.26	6,500	25,000	14.2.86
4	364/3	0.16	4,000	25,000	14.2.86
5	358	0.43	6,450	15,000	25.4.86

The land in S. No. 364/2 covered by sale No.1 was purchased for cultivation purpose. It is on the otherside of the railway track and is away from the lands under acquisition. This sale is discarded. Lands covered by sale No. 2, 3 and 4 are also situated on the other side of the track and small bits of land have been purchased for residential purposes. Hence sale Nos. 2, 3 and 4 are rejected. The land in S. No. 358 covered by sale No. 5 was purchased for the cultivation purpose and it is nearer to the lands under acquisition. It is similar to the lands under acquisition in all respect. The land acquisition officers relied on this sale. According to this sale the value of lands is Rs. 15,000 per acre. There is a time-lag of one year between the date of sale and the date of demand notice publication. The officers allowed a margin of Rs. 1000 per acre and fixed the value of land under acquisition at Rs. 16,000 per acre.

Types and Systems of Farming

Farming may be classified on the basis of similarity in (a) crop and livestock raising and (b) the mode of economic and social functioning. Based on the above factors, farming is classified into two groups:

(i) Type of farming.

(ii) System of farming.

According to Johnson System of farming refers to the combination of products on a given farm and the methods or practices that are used in the production of the product. Type of farming refers to when farms in a group are quite similar in the kinds and proportions of the crops and livestock that are produced and the methods and practices followed in production.

According to Ross: The kind of a major produce sold, forms a practical basis of classifying individual farms into system of farming. An area in which many farms have a general similarity in size, products sold and methods followed is called type of farming.

Types of farming: Farming is classified into the following types based on the enterprise and income.

1) Specialised farming

2) Diversified farming

3) Mixed farming

4) Ranching

5) Dry farming

1) SPECIALISED FARMING

A specialised farm is one on which 50% or more of income is derived from one single source. Hookin says we may best consider specialisation as the production of only one commodity for market, so that the farmer depends on a single source of income. A trend towards specialised farming is evident in areas where there are special market outlets and when economic conditions are fairly uniform for a long period.

Advantages of Specialised Farming

   a) *Better use of land*: It is more profitable to grow a crop on a land best suited to it.

   b) *Better marketing*: It allows better assembling, grading, processing, storing, transport and financing of the produce.

   c) *Better management*: The fewer enterprises on a farm are liable to be less neglected and sources of wastage can easily be detected.

   d) Less equipment and labour are needed.

   e) Costly and efficient machinery can be kept.

   f) Efficiency and skill are increased.

Disadvantages
  a) There is a greater risk of failure of crop and market together ruining the farmer.
  b) Productive resources are not fully utilised.
  c) Fertility of soil cannot be maintained.
  d) By-products of the farm cannot be fully utilised for lack of sufficient livestock on the farm.
  e) Farm returns are not generally distributed throughout the year.
  f) General knowledge of farm enterprise become limited.

2) DIVERSIFIED FARMING

A farm on which no single product source of income equals as much as 50% of the total receipts is called as diversified or general farm. On such a farm the farmers depend on several sources of income.

Advantages
  a) Better use of factors of production.
  b) Business risk is reduced.
  c) Proper utilisation of by-products.
  d) Regular and quick returns are obtained from various enterprises.

Disadvantages
  a) Market is insufficient unless the producers arrange for the sale of the produce.
  b) Because of various jobs in diversified farming, a farmer can effectively supervise only a limited number of workers.
  c) Well-equiping the farm is not possible, because it is not economical to have expensive implements and machinery for each enterprise.
  d) Changes of the leaks of farm business may remain undetected due to diversity of operations.

3) MIXED FARMING

Mixed farming is a combination of crop production with a significant amount of livestock raising. It refers to that type of diversified agriculture, in which a farmer invariably devotes to livestock production as a complementary enterprise.

The most important reason for mixed farming is that, it has been necessary in most of the regions to permit the use of a system of crop rotations combined with livestock enterprises, for getting draught animals for cultivation and also for maintaining and improving soil fertility. At least 10% of the gross income must be contributed by the livestock and the upper limit being 49% under Indian conditions. Bullocks were not considered as a part of the livestock enterprise, then even the farm can be called as mixed farming. For Indian agriculture as a whole, mixed farming is a rule.

Advantages
   a) It helps the maintenance of soil fertility.
   b) It tends to give balanced labour load throughout the year for the farmer and his family.
   c) It permits the proper use of farm by-products.
   d) It provides for greater chances of intensive cultivation.
   e) It often gets higher returns on farm business.

4) RANCHING
   A ranch differs from other types of crop and livestock, in that the livestock grazes on natural vegetation and multiply under natural surroundings. Ranch land is not utilised by tilling or raising crops. The ranches have no land of their own and make use of the public grazing land.

5) DRY FARMING
   Farmers in dry and precarious tracts which receive 20" or less of annual rainfall, struggle for livelihood. No irrigation is provided. So, farming is predominantly rainfed. The major farm management problem in these tracts, where crops are entirely dependent upon rainfall is the conservation of soil moisture.

Factors Determining the Type of Farming
   There are two kinds of factors affecting the type of farming:
Physical factors—Climate, soil, topography, etc.
Economic factors—
   1) Marketing cost
   2) Changes in relative value of farm products
   3) Availability of labour and capital
   4) Land values
   5) Cycles of over and under production
   6) Competition between enterprises
   7) Personal likes and dislikes
   8) Prevalence of pests and diseases

ECONOMIC FACTORS

Economic factors determine the crop and livestock enterprises to be taken up in a particular region within the choices established by physical factors.

1) Marketing Costs

The costs of marketing farm products and the marketing problems determine what products will or should be produced. The producer's share in consumer's price will decide the methods of sale and choice of products by the producers. A low share to the producers will cause little preference to that product in relation to high producers share.

2) Changes in Relative Value of Farm Products

The response of the production of a particular product, is much influenced by the farm product–price fluctuations and profitability, determining inturn the type of farming. Especially, the area and production of cash crops like cotton, tobacco and sugarcane, etc., are prone to changes in a cyclical manner adjusting to the price fluctuations and profitability.

3) Availability of Labour and Capital

Farm enterprises requiring intensive operations require a good amount of labour involvement and capital investment. Labour and capital intensive farming in a region brings about migration of labour from one region to the other region. For example, migration of labour on a large scale from Maharashtra to Gujarat sugarcane regions, and from Andhra Pradesh to Maharastra sugarcane regions is a common feature.

4) Land Value

Low land values attract the enterprising farmers from high land value areas, to settle and develop a new type of farming in those areas. Due to this new type of farming, low land values will go up in the course of time. For example, farmers from coastal Andhra Pradesh purchasing low value lands in parts of Karnataka and other parts of Andhra Pradesh, where they had introduced cotton farming and rice farming on an intensive scale.

5) Cycles of Over and Under-production

Agricultural enterprises are frequently subject to cycles of over and under-production, resulting in surplus/scarcity of production and low/high prices. This results in speculation and uncertainty in the type of crops to be grown. As a result, farmers prefer to grow such crops whose prices are on the rise or stable. This phenomenon gives rise to the Cob-Web Theorem. Frequent fluctuations in the production of cash crops like cotton, tobacco, etc., in a cyclical manner is a common feature in India.

6) Competition between Enterprises

Specialisation or diversification of farming is decided by the competition among the enterprises depending upon their relative profitability and resources use competition.

7) Personal Likes and Dislikes of the Farming Groups

The type of farming or choice of products sometimes is determined by the personal preferences of the farmers, either due to traditional values or attachments they had in that particular crop.

8) Prevalence of Pests and Diseases

The occurrence of pests and diseases on an endemic fashion in a region will ruin or extinguish the entire type of farming and gives rise to new type of farming. In Guntur and Prakasam districts of Andhra Pradesh during 1984-85, 1985-86, the attack of white fly on cotton caused a 40 per cent decrease in cotton farming area. The cultivation of pulse crops and oilseed crops emerged as a new type of farming in this cotton belt.

Systems of Farming

The term systems of farming is generally referred to the methods of agriculture and the type of ownership of land. If the farming has been classified on the basis of economic and social functioning, it is called as systems of farming.

1) CO-OPERATIVE FARMING

A co-operative farming means a system under which all agricultural operations or part of them are carried on jointly by the farmers on a voluntary basis, each farmer retaining the right on his own land. The farmers would pool their land, labour and capital. The land would be treated as one unit and cultivated jointly under the direction of an elected management.

A part of the profit would be distributed in proportion to the land contributed by each farmer and the rest of the profit would be distributed in proportion to the wages earned by each farmer.

Co-operative farming societies are of four different types:

a) Co-operative Better Farming

Under this system, the land is not pooled and cultivation is carried out by each farmer separately. Here the ownership and operationship both are individual.

It promotes the interest of the members through the adoption of better farming practices. It arranges for the purchase of seeds, manure, joint use of machinery, etc.

A member is free to follow his own way of farming, except in respect of the purpose for which he joins the society, e.g., irrigation, purchase of seeds, marketing of produce, etc.

b) Co-operative Joint Farming

Under this system, the ownership is individual and the operationship is collective, the land of the members is pooled for joint cultivation. Ownership of each member over his land is recognised by payment of a dividend in proportion to the value of his land. The members work on the land under the direction of a managing committee and each member receives wages for his daily labour.

c) Co-operative Tenant Farming

Under this system the ownership is collective and the operationship is individual. The land is held by the society and not by the members individually. The land is then divided into plots, which are leased out for cultivation to individual members. The society arranges for the agricultural requirements, e.g. credit, seeds, manures, marketing of produce, etc. Each member is responsible to the society for payment of the rent of his plots, and is at liberty to dispose off his produce in such a manner as he likes.

d) Co-operative Collective Farming

Under this system, the operationship is collective and ownership is also collective. The land is owned by the society and cultivation is done jointly. The method of work of the society is similar to that of a co-operative joint farming society. But the right of share of individual members on the land is not recognised. The profits are paid to the members in proportion to the work and capital contributed by each member.

2) COLLECTIVE FARMING

In collective farming, members of collectives surrender their land, livestock and deadstock to the society, the collectives cannot refuse to admit other members of required qualification.

The members work together under a management committee elected by themselves. The committee directs farm management in matters of allocation of work, distribution of income and marketing surplus and puts all members into labour to see that the work is done efficiently. The main source of income is through labour earnings.

3) CAPITALIST FARMING

This type of farming based on capitalistic methods where landlordism exist as in America or England. The role of capital is more, wage labour use is more than family labour under this farming. In India, this type of farming can be seen in commercialised agricultural areas, where farm production is market and profit oriented. In such farms, improved methods of agriculture are followed and the application of capital input is high, because the landlords happen to be a capitalist and non-cultivating owner provide necessary fixed and working capital.

4) STATE FARMING

Under this system, farms are managed by government officials. The workers are paid wages on weekly or monthly basis. In India, all states farms are governed by an independent body, i.e. State Farms Corporation. Various activities of research can be facilitated under state farming.

5) PEASANT FARMING

The peasant farming farmers follow agricultural practices in their own way and are managers and organisers of their farm business. Living and working are closely related. The entire farm family of the farmer has a part in making decisions and executing the farming programme.

The members of the family are actively associated with some of the phases of the farm business, particularly with the care of the livestock and looking after the kitchen garden and poultry, if any.

The peasants effectively increase the family labour force during busy seasons of sowing and harvesting for a short time, by working longer hours and by working faster. Thus the peasant farming on the one hand places a high premium on management and the use of family labour, which maximise farm business income and on the other allows the organisation of the farm to be adjusted to the capabilities of the various members of the family.

Systems of farming	Type of ownership	Type of Operationship
1. (a) Cooperative better farming	Individual	Individual
(b) Cooperative joint farming	Individual	Collective
(c) Cooperative tenant farming	Collective	Individual
(d) Cooperative collective farming	Collective	Collective
2. Collective-farming	Society or State	Society or State
3. Capitalist farming	Individual	Individual
4. State farming	State	Paid management
5. Peasant farming	Individual	Individual

Farm Labour Management

CLASSIFICATION OF FARM LABOUR

Farm Labour is classified into:

1) Unpaid labour
2) Paid labour (Hired)

Unpaid labour is further classified into:

1) Farmer's own labour
2) Family labour

Paid labour is further classified into:

a) Permanent or attached labour
b) Casual-hired labour or seasonal labour.

Paid labour is also classified as skilled and unskilled labour.

Farm manager's labour, farm family's labour and permanent hired labour are fixed resources due to general lack of mobility. Casual labour is a variable input.

Farm Manager's Labour

Indian farmer is a manager. Managers' labour is of course the best type of available labour due to his personal interest; though Indian farmer is a comparatively good labourer, he remains to be an inefficient farm organiser and a poor capitalist. Family labour is the main source of labour on Indian farms.

Permanent Hired Labour

It is hired on cash, kind or crop share basis for a fixed period. Six months or one year.

Casual Labour

It is hired from time-to-time and according to the demand for agricultural operations. Demand being seasonal only, there is always a mal-adjustment in the supply of and demand for agricultural labour. Peak workload period supply cannot meet the demand. In the slack seasons, there are too many labourers seeking employment.

Skilled Labour

Specialised labour and trained labour for specific jobs is known as skilled labour. Semi-skilled labour does not require any elaborate training and does the job which cannot be taken up by ordinary labourer.

Unskilled Labour

It is ordinary labour employed for manual work, which does not need any training of specialised nature.

Special Features of Indian Farm Labour
1) Mostly under-employed
2) Disguised unemployment
3) Growing average size of labour families
4) Low productivity
5) Lack of organisation
6) Low bargaining power and low standard of living
7) Low wages and seasonal nature of employment.

Farm Wages

Farm wages are of three kinds:
1) Time basis
2) Piece basis
3) Share basis

The minimum rates of wages payable to each category of casual labour employed in agriculture in the state of Andhra Pradesh with effect from 9-2-1987 for six hours working in a day, except for ploughing which is five hours in a day, the following rates are applicable to men and women equally. Young persons in the age group of 15 to 18 years and who are certified for child work only, shall be paid 80 per cent of wages fixed for adult workers for that category. The rates vary from zone to zone in the state, with the maximum and minimum rates.

		Wages per day (Rs.)	
		Maximum	Minimum
a)	Ploughing	14.50	9.60
b)	Threshing	15.00	10.20
c)	Sowing		
d)	Transplanting	12.00	9.60
e)	Harvesting		
f)	Weeding		
g)	Any other light operation not involving skill or hazard	11.00	8.50
h)	Digging		
i)	Stacking	14.40	9.00
j)	Pruning		
k)	Spraying of pesticides	21.60	14.20
l)	Tobacco pluckers	18.00	16.20
m)	Mali	14.40	9.00
n)	Watchman	18.00	11.00

Labour Management

The following points are to be considered under labour management:

1) Preparation of labour calendar to know approximately the total labour requirements of crops and livestock enterprises at various seasons on the farm. Calculation of peak labour needs of crops and crop cultivation and plan for meeting the needs through adjustment in crop plans.
2) Making suitable arrangements for the employment of hired and family labour during slack season.
3) Planning work for rainy day to employ the hired labour on indoor jobs.
4) Adjustment of crop and livestock programme to meet the problem of shortage of labour.
5) Time and motion study to engage labour efficiently.

THE EFFICIENCY OF LABOUR

Labour efficiency in agriculture refers to the amount of productive work accomplished per man on the farm per unit of time.

The efficiency of labour depends upon:

1) The physical conditions of labour and interest taken by him in his work.

2) The kind of tools, implements and equipment which he uses.
3) The conditions under which he is working.
4) The skill with which he works.

MEASURES OF LABOUR EFFICIENCY
   1) Marginal analysis in a specific situation,
   2) Conventional measures, and
   3) Labour efficiency index.

1) Marginal Productivity Analysis

Marginal productivity is the output produced by an additional unit of labour input. Average productivity of labour is the output per unit of labour.

2) Conventional Measures

a) Where labour is a scarce factor, the hectares of crops per man is considered a good measure.

$$\text{It is calculated as} = \frac{\text{Total work units}}{\text{Man equivalents}}$$

This indicates the number of days of productive work done by a worker on the farm in crop production, dairying or any other enterprise, e.g. number of cows per man or amount of milk produced or sold per man and number of egg laying hens per man.

The different kinds of workers—men, women and children are converted into man equivalent, i.e. 2 men = 3 women and 1 man = 2 children.

$$\text{b) Return per labour day} = \frac{\text{Family labour income}}{\text{No. of family labour days}}$$

$$\text{c) Out-turn per worker} = \frac{\text{Average output by the average number of earners}}{\text{Average number of adult male family members (earners)}}$$

$$\text{d) Return per worker} = \frac{\text{Value of output minus cost of input factors excluding human labour}}{\text{Total number of workers}}.$$

3) Labour Efficiency Index

In areas where labour efficiency standards have been set on the basis of the amount of labour to be performed on crops and livestock, the labour efficiency can be worked out.

Suppose the labour required for a given farm is calculated at 5,000 units of work on crops and 2,500 units on livestock. The normal labour cost for such a combination is Rs. 2,000 but the actual labour cost is Rs. 2,500. The efficiency index is calculated as:

$$\frac{\text{Rs. 2,000}}{\text{Rs. 2,500}} \times 100 = 80\%$$

i.e. the efficiency is below normal (100).

$$\text{Expressed as percentage of normal cost} = \frac{\text{Rs. 2,500}}{\text{Rs. 2,000}} \times 100 = 125\%$$

i.e. the cost is above normal (100).

MEASURES OF INCREASING THE FARM LABOUR EFFICIENCY
1) Enlarge the size of the farm business
2) Planning labour distribution—enterprise combination
3) Improve the field and farm layout
4) Improving the farm buildings programme
5) Improved labour management with planning of the work, incentives and training of the workers
6) Farm work simplification
7) Fixing efficiency standards for various types of work

FARM WORK SIMPLIFICATION
Farm work simplication or job analysis is a promising method of reducing farm labour requirements. Its objective is a more efficient use of labour and other resources by improving work methods, so that more and higher quality work is accomplished in less time and with less energy.

Savings in time and energy are of particular importance. Farm work simplification consists of breaking each operation into its constituent parts and then examining each part carefully to determine:

1) Whether that particular part of the work is really necessary or could either be omitted or combined with some other job.
2) Whether the method could be simplified, so that time and money could be saved.
3) Avoid unnecessary trips and duplications.
4) Whether tools and equipment are of the most efficient type and size.

Answers to these following questions will help the efficient organisation of labour.

1) Why is it necessary?
2) Where should it be done?
3) When should it be done?
4) Who should do it?
5) What is the best way to do it?

Planning Through Enterprise Combinations

Though Indian agriculture is fairly diversified, yet the employment of labour is not regular or constant throughout the year. There are some peak work-load periods and a few slack months. This leads to low level of labour efficiency. If different crop enterprises are planned, such that as far as possible peak and slacks are reduced, labour efficiency will improve. Addition of dairy cattle or poultry, to crop farming can thus absorb surplus labour in this slack season.

Management of Capital Equipment

Machinery and equipment is the major component of fixed capital on farms and there is a large variety of machines and equipment from which every farmer has to choose, within the framework of his farm organisation, in order to reduce per-unit costs in the long run and achieve the highest returns per unit of time. The management of mechanisation on the farms are reduced drudgery on tedious operations, reduced costs, increased returns through increasing the intensity, efficiency and timeliness of operations. Once it is decided to get the work done with the machine, the immediate management question is whether to own the machine or to get it on custom-hiring. Again, if it is to be owned, what should be its size and whether it should be new or second-hand.

The key points to consider while deciding upon the size of a machine are:

1) The difference in the initial cost of the large and small machines.
2) The annual use to be made of the machine.
3) The amount of additional labour saved by the machine.
4) The relative opportunity cost of capital and labour on the farm.

The labour saved by the machine and the relative values of labour and machinery in a given farm are the key considerations, because labour and machinery are substitutable.

Substituting Machinery for Labour

In order to lower the costs, machinery should be substituted for labour when the labour saved is more than the increase in machine costs. The substitution can take place when, (1) changing from hand to machine method, (2) changing types of machines and (3) increasing the size of machine.

DETERMINING THE PROFITABILITY OF A MACHINE

Buying a machine or other equipment depends upon whether the profits would be higher after the machine is introduced into farm organisation or not. Thus, it involves evaluation of the entire set of changes that would occur, once the machine is owned. Savings in labour costs, increase in cropping area, returns, improvement in timeliness of operations and the associated increase in yield, should be to the credit of machine management.

The appraisal of profitability of the machine should always be based on the opportunity costs. Custom-hiring versus owning a machine, second hand machine versus a new one, labour versus machine power, alternatives of mechanising a particular operation. The returns on capital from buying the machine should be compared with the returns from alternative investments that can be made with the same capital. The evaluation of profitability of a particular machine or equipment, can be put in the format of a partial budget.

The evaluation of a machine or capital equipment involves the consideration of the following items.

Debit (Added costs and reduced returns)	Credit (Added returns and reduced costs)
1) Fixed costs of the machine	1) Fixed cost of equipment replaced
2) Increase in fuel and repairs costs	2) Decrease in fuel and repair costs
3) Increase in input costs	3) Labour costs saved
4) Returns from decreased yields	4) Other input materials saved
5) Decrease in returns from the replaced crops	5) Returns from increased yields and/or price premium for quality product
6) Risk factors	6) Returns from increased acreage under more paying crops and/or new crops

7) Increase in returns from
   more cropped area
8) Leisure preference

BREAK-EVEN POINT FOR MACHINERY

The important management decision, as to when to leave or abandon one practice and start another, i.e. effect a change in the system is answered by the break-even point. Break-even point refers to that volume of business, at which the farmer is indifferent between two alternatives, i.e. he is neither better-off nor worse-off irrespective of the choice he makes. Break-even point is a point of indecision or the crucial point, on the scale of decision.

The break-even level is given by the point where the fixed costs are covered (Fig.6.1) and only beyond that, the farmer can make profits.

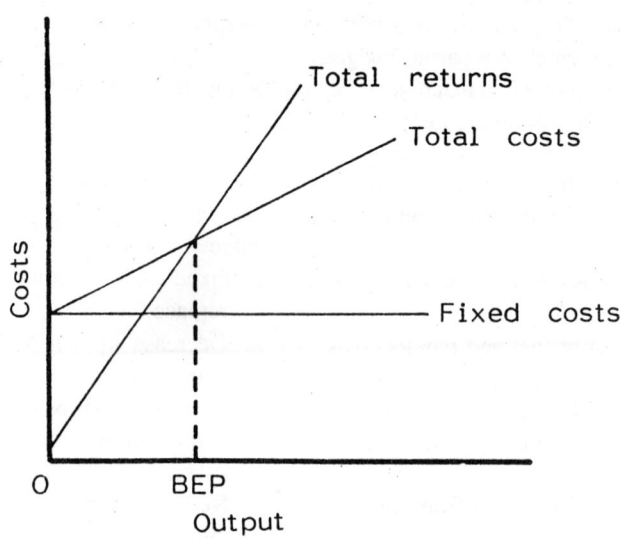

Fig. 6.1. Break-even level of output.

Suppose a farmer wants to buy a seed-cum-fertiliser drill with a capital cost of Rs. 2,000. He normally grows 15 acres of the crop, for which the machine is bought. He will save on some costs, say labour, but will have to incur more on some other items, say fuel. The net increase in variable costs per acre comes to say Rs. 10, although he achieves timeliness and better operational efficiency, he cannot be sure of what extra yields he will obtain. With this information, we can work out break-even increase in yields required to justify the purchase of drill. Suppose the machine lasts for 10 years, the annual depreciation comes to Rs. 200; the average annual interest on capital at 12% is Rs. 120 and the annual repair costs are, say Rs. 40. Thus the annual fixed costs are Rs. 360. The break-even yield can be worked out as follows:

Price of input × increase in yield per acre × No. of acres

= Annual total fixed costs + (variable costs per acre × No. of acres).

If the output is valued at Rs. 68 per quintal and the farmer grows 15 acres as usual, the above equation becomes:

$$68 \times \text{increase in yield per acre} \times 15 = 360 + 10 \times 15$$

$$\text{or break-even increase in yield} = \frac{360 + (10 \times 15)}{68 \times 15}$$

$$= 0.5 \text{ quintal/acre.}$$

Similarly, break-even acreage or the break-even price can be worked out.

CHAPTER 7

Farm Business Analysis

Farm business analysis is the name given to a technique based on computation and interpretation of a variety of efficiency measures for the farm under study. The results of the analysis are then compared with standards derived from a group of farms of a similar size and type. This comparison is used to highlight organisational weaknesses and strengths of the farm business.

If farm accounts are available, this system of farm business analysis can be a useful tool. The subject of farm business analysis is dealt with under different names, i.e. Farm Accountancy, Farm Records and Accounts or Farm Book Keeping. The objective is the same and the difference lies in the methods of treatment or approaches.

Farm Accountancy is defined as the art as well as the science of recording in books the business transactions in a regular and systematic manner, so that their nature, extent and financial effects can be readily ascertained at any time of the year.

Farm Book Keeping is known as a system of records written to furnish a history of the business transactions, with special reference to its financial side (Adams). Farm accounting thus, in the usual sense is an application of the accounting principles to the business of farming.

The objective of Farm Records and Accounts is to provide control over the business and improve the management of the farm.

Farm Records and Accounts

With the help of farm records, the farmer knows:
1) Which enterprises ar e making profit or loosing money, i.e. to check on performance of different enterprises.
2) Which enterprises are returning most over his capital investment.
3) To guide future decisions.
4) Whether to go in for specialisation or diversification.
5) To provide planning data for use in making or revising future plans.
6) Whether addition of new activities will boost the rate of return on his capital.

Farm records should reveal the strengths in a business that can be exploited and the weaknesses that must be removed.

Farm records help existing labour and capital returns for the various practices and enterprises and provide the basis for comparison with new ones which might be used. Farm records provide details on the previous year's operations, showing which enterprise gave the greatest return on capital, as well as the degree of technical and economic efficiency attained in the various business aspects.

Farm records not only indicate progress made in crop yields, livestock efficiency and return on investment, but they also show progress in capital accumulation, net worth and in general efficiency in management. New directions can be determined to fit into alternative plans. So farm records are to be maintained to judge the farming efficiency and profitability of farming.

CHARACTERISTICS OF GOOD RECORD SYSTEM

1) Easy to keep and be up to date.
2) Give needed information for analysis.
3) Provide the information when needed and serve a definite purpose.
4) Permit the analysis of the information needed.

ADVANTAGES OF FARM RECORDS AND ACCOUNTS

1) Means to higher income
2) Basis for diagnosis and planning
3) Way to improve the managerial ability of the farmer
4) Basis for credit acquisition and management
5) Guide to better management and future decisions
6) Basis for research
7) Basis for policy formulation

PROBLEMS AND DIFFICULTIES IN FARM ACCOUNTING IN INDIA

1) Subsistence nature of farming
2) Triple role of Indian farmer and difficulties of maintenance, farm manager, farm labour and family head
3) Illiteracy and lack of business awareness
4) Complicated nature of agri-business
5) Inadequate extension service in making farmers record oriented
6) Non-availability of suitable and simplified farm record books under Indian conditions
7) Lack of record consciousness
8) Fear of taxation

SYSTEMS OF BOOK KEEPING

There are Two Systems of Farm Accountancy
1) Double-entry system
2) Single-entry system

Double-entry system
It is a method of recording each transaction in the books of accounts in its two-fold aspects, i.e. two entries are made for each transaction, in the same set of books; one being a *debit entry* and the other a *credit entry*. It involves two parties—one for receiving the goods or services and the other for giving them.

Example 1
a) Sale of paddy for Rs. 240
Cash account and paddy account—two accounts
b) Cash a/c receiving account—hence the amount written on debit side of it
c) Paddy a/c giving account—hence the amount will be written on credit side of it.

Example 2
Receipt of money from Mr. Prasad Rs. 250
Cash account received—Debitor
Prasad paid the amount—Credit to Prasad's amount.

Single-entry system
This is the system which ignores the double effect of transactions. Only personal accounts of debitors and creditors are kept and impersonal accounts are ignored altogether.

Types of Farm Records
Farm records system consists of three parts:
1) Physical farm records
2) Financial farm records
3) Supplementary farm records

PHYSICAL FARM RECORDS
To implement the financial records and financial decisions, the physical data recording concerning the farm and its performance are essential. The uses of farm records, earlier assets are: to check performance of

enterprises, for controlling the business; to aid the analysis of past results, to detect weaknesses and strengths to guide future decisions; and to provide planning data. As the prices of both outputs and inputs are subject to continuous fluctuations, the physical data recording is in many ways, of greater importance than the financial information. The following are the physical records that should be kept.

1) Farm map
2) Land utilisation records
3) Production and disposal record for crops, livestock, poultry and others
4) Labour records
5) Machinery use records
6) Feed records
7) Stock and store register

FINANCIAL RECORDS

In order to provide information regarding the profitability of the whole farm business over a given period, the financial records are important to be maintained. They enable the analysis to be carried out to reveal the economic strengths and weaknesses of the farming system, and to provide data to help in the preparation of revised plans and budgets. The following financial records should be kept.

1) Farm inventory
2) Farm cash or farm financial record
3) Classified farm cash account and annual business analysis
4) Capital asset and sale register
5) Cash sale register
6) Credit sale register
7) Purchase register
8) Wage register
9) Funds borrowed and repayment register
10) Farm expenses paid in kind register
11) Non-farm income record

SUPPLEMENTARY RECORDS

a) Sanction register
b) Auction register
c) Rainfall register
d) Hire register
e) Stationary register

AN EXAMPLE OF SIMPLIFIED FARM BOOK KEEPING TO
INDIAN FARMERS IS PRESENTED BELOW

Farm Record Book   Year: 1987–88

1) Name of the Farmer : Sri Karri Satyanarayana Rao
2) Village   : Kavitam
3) Taluk/Mandal   : Poduru
4) District   : West Godavari
5) Farm Inventory   :
    a)   Land (owned and leased): 4.12ha.
        i)   Survey no:
        ii) Identification of the plot:
    East :   Pond of 5.45 ha belongs to Panchayat
    South: Field of Sri Velagala Sree Rami Reddy
    West :   Yanamaduru Drain, which flows north to south
    North: Field of Sri G. Prabhakara Reddy
        iii) Soil type and texture : Black clayey soils with compact
            texture
        iv) Type of tenure (owned/leased/leased in): Owned
        v)   Source of irrigation: Nidadavole - Narsapur canal of Go-
            davari Western Delta
        vi) Area of the plot (ha): 4.12
            Irrigated   : 4.12
            Unirrigated : —
            Irrigated dry : —
            Total   : 4.12
        vii) Present value of land (Rs.): 8,45,000
        viii) Rental value (Rs.): No
    ix) Remarks: The government rate will be very less.

    b) Farm building and other structures

Sl. No.	Description	Type of construction	Year of construction/ purchase	Value at the time of construction/ purchase	Expected life	Remarks
i)	Dwelling house	Pucca	1958	Rs. 45,000	100 years	—
ii)	Cattle shed	Tiled roof without any concrete cover on floor	1981	Rs. 13,000	75 years	—
iii)	Storage shed	—	—	—	—	—
iv)	Others	—	—	—	—	—

c) Wells, tube-wells, pumpsets and related irrigation structure

Sl. No.	Item	Description	Year of construction/ purchase	Cost of construction/ purchase	Value at the beginning of the year (Rs.)	Expected life	Remarks
i)	Filter point	Tube well	1958	Rs. 250	Rs. 1,000	35 years	—

d) Implements and machinery

Sl. No.	Description	No.	Year of making or purchase	If purchased-price (Rs.)	Value at the beginning of the year (Rs.)	Expected life	Remarks
i)	*Implements*						
	Spades	6	1985	90	72	10	—
	Crowbars	2	1986	40	50	30	—
	Sickles	6	1987	90	60	10	—
	Wooden planks	2	1985	50	30		—
ii)	*Machinery*						
	Sprayer (Knapsack)	1	1977	450	250	20	—
iii)	*Transport equipment* Nil	—	—	—	—	—	—
iv)	*Others to be Specified*						
	Winnowing baskets	25	1986–87	125	100	2	—

e) Livestock

Sl. No.	Description	No.	Bread	Home bread or purchased	Year of purchase	Price at which purchased	Present market value	Remarks
i)	Breeding animals Nil	—	—	—	—	—	—	—
ii)	Drought animals Nil	—	—	—	—	—	—	—
iii)	Milch animals							
	Buffaloes	2	Murrah	Purchased	1985	4,000	3,500	—
	Calves	4	Murrah	Home bread	—	—	500	—
iv)	Others	—	—	—	—	—	—	—
v)	Total	6	—	—	—	4,000	4,000	—

f) Changes in the inventory during the year

Date	Addition				Date	Reduction				Remarks
	Description	Mode of addition	No./Qty	Value		Description	Mode of disposal	No./Qty	Value	
24.02.87	Sickles	To replace the old wear sickles	6	90	18.12.87	Old sickles	—	5	50	
06.05.87	Winnowing baskets	For the winnowing	25	125	21.07.87	She buffalo	Sold	1	2100.	
18.06.87	Levelling the field to cover the pits formed due to tractor ploughing	Filling the pits	—	68	10.09.87	Winnowing baskets	Teared	18	40	
22.06.87	New bunds formation in middle of the field as it is uneven	Bund formation	—	34						
							Balance		1900	

6) Crop Production Records

Date	Name of the produce	Area from which obtained (ha)	Identity of plot	Main product		By-product		Remarks
				Quantity (Qtls)	Value	Quantity (tonnes)	Value	
14.12.86	Paddy (*Kharif*)	4.12	East : Pond West : Drain South : Field of Sir VSR Reddy North : Field of Sri GP Reddy	214.50	28,600	13	1,300	
02.04.87	Paddy (*Rabi*)	4.12	East : Pond West : Drain South : Field of Sir VSR Reddy North : Field of Sri GP Reddy	263.25	35,100	17	1,700	

7) Fodder and Feed for Cattle

Date (monthly)	Type of livestock	Type of fodder	Owned/ purchased	Fodder fed		Concentrates		Remarks
				Qty.	Value	Qty.	Value	
Dec – March	Buffaloes(2)	Rice bran *Dolichos biflorus*	Purchased	400 kg	750	75 kg	95	
July – Oct.	Calves	Horsegram	Purchased	120 kg	105	—	—	
	Buffaloes(2)	Grass	Owned	800 kg	200	—	—	
Apr – May	Calves(2)	*Pillipesara*	Owned	1200 kg	600	—	—	

8) Disposal of Produce from Crops

Name of the produce	Disposal agency	Sales		Payment in kind		Other disposals			Remarks
		Qty. (Qtls)	Value (Rs.)	Qty. (Qtls)	Value (Rs.)	Type	Qty. (Qtls)	Value (Rs.)	
Paddy (*Kharif*)	Middleman	154.50	20,600	7.5 (Permanent labour)	1000	For Seed	15	4000	
						For Home consumption	45	6000	
Paddy (*Rabi*)	Middleman	225.75	32,100	7.5 (for labour)	1000	Seed	15	4000	

9) Receipts Other than Sales of Farm Produce (Cash and Kind)

Date	Source of receipts	Cash receipts (Rs.)	Kind Receipts			Total (Rs.)	Remarks
			Type of commodity	Qty. of commodity	Value		
	Milk	2,440	—	—	—	2,440	

10) Cropping Pattern
    a) Survey number :
    b) Identification of the plot:
       East   :   Pond belongs to Panchayat of Kavitam
       West   :   Yanamaduru drain
       South   :   The field of Sri V. Sree Rami Reddy
       North   :   The field of Sri G. Prabhakar Reddy
    c) Area of the plot (ha)
       i)   Cultivated area   :   4.12
       ii) Uncultivated area   :   —
       iii) Reasons   :   The land is wet with full of
                                      irrigation facilities
    d) Season - I
       i)   Crop name   :   Paddy (*Kharif*)
       ii) Variety   :   MTU 5249, MTU 2077
       iii) Area under the crop:
            Irrigated   :   4.12
            Total   :   4.12
    e) Season - II
       i)   Crop name   :   Paddy (*Rabi*)
       ii) Variety   :   IR-64, IET-1444, BPT-1235
       iii) Area under the crop:
            Irrigated   :   4.12
            Total   :   4.12
    f) Remarks: Only monoculture of paddy has been practiced

11) Milk Production and Disposal of Livestock Produce
    a) Date   : 27-09-1987
    b) Identification of animal : Buffalo with white spot on the fore-
       head
    c) Milk yield in litres:
       i)   Morning   : 3 litres
       ii) Evening   : 3 litres
    d) Disposal agency: : —
    e) Quantity (milk)   : 6 litres
    f) Value   : Rs. 24
    g) Home consumption (Qty): 4 litres
       2 litres for selling to neighbours @ Rs. 4 per litre
    h) Others (Hides & Skin, etc.)
       i)   Type   : —

ii)	Disposal	:	—
iii)	Agency	:	—
iv)	Quantity	:	—
v)	Value	:	—

12) Feeds and Production from Other Enterprises (Poultry, Piggery, etc., and their disposal)

a)	Date	:	—
b)	Type of enterprise	:	—
c)	Feed		
	i) Type	:	—
	ii) Quantity	:	—
	iii) Value	:	—
d)	Production	:	Nil
	i) Type	:	—
	ii) Quantity	:	—
	iii) Value	:	—
e)	Disposa		
	i) Disposal	:	—
	ii) Agency	:	—
	iii) Quantity	:	—
	iv) Value	:	—
f)	Home consumption (Qty)	:	—

13) Record of Loans

a)	Date of transaction	20-6-1987
b)	Loan taken	—
	i) Type of loan	Crop loan
	ii) Purpose for which loan taken	Purchase of fertilisers
	iii) Agency providing the loan	Andhra Bank
	iv) Amount of the loan	Rs. 5,000
	v) Rate of interest per annum	11.5% per annum
c)	Repayment of loans :	Nil
	i) Agency to which repayment made —	
	ii) Amount (Rs.)	—
d)	Loans outstanding:	Nil
	i) Principal	—
	ii) Interest	—
e)	Remarks (Indicate overdue)	—

Farm Inventory Analysis

Farm inventory is a list of all the physical properties of a business along with their value at a specific date. It is a complete list of farmer's assets with their valuation at a point of time.

An inventory repeated at another point of time would account for the depreciation or appreciation of the assets and their sale or purchase during the period between the inventories.

The difference between two inventories reflects the profit or loss during that period. Usually the period refers to an agricultural year and the inventory at the beginning of the year is compared with that at the end of the year.

Assets: An asset is a physical property or intangible right owned by a business or an individual that have a value.

Assets are classified into the following types:

(1) Fixed assets, (2) Working assets, (3) Current assets.

1) FIXED ASSETS

They are of the nature that it is difficult to convert them into cash to meet any current obligations. For example land, buildings and other long lived inventory structures.

2) WORKING ASSETS

They are more liquid than fixed assets, such as farm machinery and equipment, etc. for example, breeding and producing livestock. These resources will ordinarily be worn out in the normal process of business. Their value may be regarded as being transferred slowly to the products of the farm operations.

3) CURRENT ASSETS

These consists of cash on hand, bills recoverable, crops, feed on hand, livestock that is or will shortly be in condition for sale. Current assets may be considered as assets which in the normal operation of the business will be liquidated within the accounting year.

Methods of Valuation

1) Cost minus depreciation
2) Cost or market price whichever is lower
3) Net selling price
4) Replacement cost minus depreciation
5) Income capitalisation method

1) COST MINUS DEPRECIATION

This method assumes that the purchase price was an approximation of the value of the asset and its value in subsequent years can be determined by subtracting a depreciation allowance from its cost. It is commonly used for working assets like machinery and breeding livestock.

2) COST OR MARKET PRICE

Valuation is estimated at the cost or the market price, whichever is lower. This method is commonly used for valuing purchased farm supplies.

3) VALUATION AT NET SELLING PRICE

This means the price which could probably be obtained for the asset, if marketed, less the cost of marketing. This conform most closely to the present worth. This method is used for those items that are held primarily for the sale: crops or livestock produced for the market.

Net selling price = market price less the selling costs.

4) VALUATION BY REPLACEMENT COST MINUS DEPRECIATION

This method is to valuate the assets at what it would cost to reproduce them at present prices, and under present method of production. For example, long lived assets, like buildings. This method will guard against under-valuation, but may not ensure against over-valuation.

5) VALUATION BY INCOME—CAPITALISATION METHOD

This method is appropriate for the farm assets, whose contribution to the income of the farm business can be measured and which have a long life. The capitalisation formula = $V = I/r$ can be used for this purpose, where V = value in rupees; I = constant income over infinite number of years in future (net income per year) and r = rate of interest.

DEPRECIATION: The decline in value of capital equipment due to wear and tear is called depreciation. It is caused by two factors—time and use. As depreciation continues, the serviceability and value of the asset diminishes.

Wherever any machine or equipment performs useful work, its wear and tear is bound to occur. Its efficiency also reduces with the lapse of time, and at one time it becomes uneconomical to be used further and needs replacement by another new unit. So some money must be set aside every year from the profits, so that when that equipment becomes uneconomical, it can be replaced by the new one. Therefore, the initial cost of machine plus installation charges plus repair charges minus scrap value is charged against over heads and spread over the machine's useful life. For this purpose, depreciation charges are added in the total costs of farm products.

Depreciation can be classified as under:

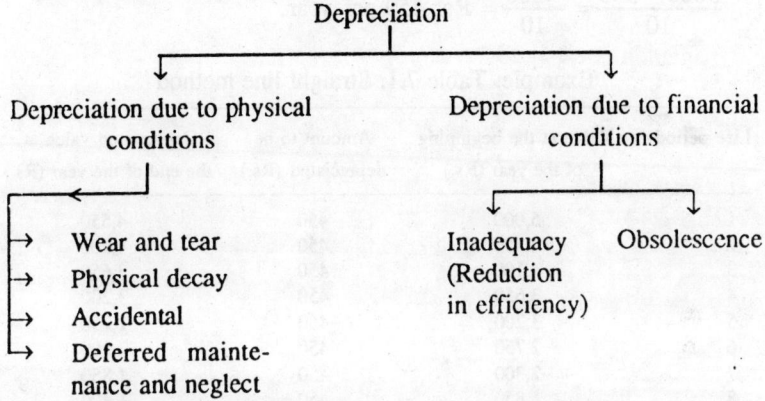

Methods of computation of depreciation
1) Straight line method
2) Annual revaluation method
3) Diminishing balance method
4) Sum of the year—Digits method (or) Reducing Fraction method
5) Compound interest methods
    a) Sinking fund method
    b) annuity charging method
6) Insurance policy method
7) Machine hour-basis method

1) STRAIGHT LINE METHOD

This method is easy, simple and usually very satisfactory for most purposes. This method assumes that assets are used more or less to the same extent every year and therefore, equal amounts of costs on account of their use can be charged every year.

$$\text{Annual Depreciation} = \frac{\text{Original cost} - \text{Junk value}}{\text{Expected life of the asset}}$$
(No. of useful years of life)

Junk value is otherwise also called as scrap value, salvage value or residual value. The purchase price minus junk value is also known as total anticipated depreciation.

For example, a bullock cart costs Rs. 5000 and is expected to last for 10 years. the salvage value after 10 years = Rs. 500. Then the annual depreciation is:

$$\frac{5000 - 500}{10} = \frac{4500}{10} = \text{Rs. } 450 \text{ per year.}$$

Example: Table 7.1. Straight line method

Life period	Value at the beginning of the year (Rs.)	Amount to be depreciated (Rs.)	Depreciated value at the end of the year (Rs.)
1	5,000	450	4,550
2	4,550	450	4,100
3	4,100	450	3,650
4	3,650	450	3,200
5	3,200	450	2,750
6	2,750	450	2,300
7	2,300	450	1,850
8	1,850	450	1,400
9	1,400	450	950
10	950	450	500

2) ANNUAL REVALUATION METHOD

This method estimates the market value of the asset in the beginning and the end of the year and then taking the difference as depreciation. This method is however useful in case of livestock in the early years of life, i.e. in appreciating phase. For items not bought and sold frequently, it becomes difficult.

3) DIMINISHING BALANCE METHOD

A fixed rate of depreciation is used for every year and applied to the value of the asset at the beginning of the year. The original cost of an asset is divided by its estimated life to knock off a fixed percentage. This percentage is deducted every year from the diminished balance, till the asset reached the salvage value and no further depreciation is possible. Suppose a machine is purchased for Rs. 1000 and its expected life is 10 years.

First year:
The annual depreciation would be:

$$\frac{\text{Original cost}}{\text{Expected life}} = \frac{\text{Rs. } 1000}{10} = \text{Rs. } 100$$

Rs. 100 is 10% of Rs. 1000.

This 10% i.e. Rs. 100 is deducted from the value.

∴Rs. 1000 – Rs.100 = Rs. 900

∴The depreciation is Rs. 100 and the depreciated value of the machine at the end of the first year would be Rs. 900.

Second year:

The amount of depreciation would be 10% of diminished balance value of the asset, i.e. Rs. 900.

10% of Rs. 900 = Rs. 90

Depreciated value of the machine at the end of second year
= Rs. 900 – Rs. 90 = Rs. 810

Third Year:

The amount of depreciation would be 10% of Rs. 810 = Rs. 81.

The depreciated value of the machine at the end of the third year would be Rs. 810 – Rs. 81 = Rs. 729.

Like the above procedure, the amount of depreciation is deducte' every year from the diminished balance value of the asset, till it reache< its salvage value.

The amount of depreciation is different at different stages of the machine and gradually diminishes with the life.

Example: Table 7.2. Diminishing balance method

Years of life	Value at the beginning of the year (Rs.)	Amount to be depreciated (10% of diminished value) (Rs.)	Depreciated value at the end of the year (Diminished balance value) (Rs.)
1	1,000	100.00	900.00
2	900	90.00	810.00
3	810	81.00	729.00
4	729.00	72.90	656.10
5	656.10	65.61	590.49
6 ∴	590.49	59.05	531.44
7	531.44	53.14	478.30
8	478.30	47.83	430.47
9	430.47	43.05	387.42
10	387.42	38.74	348.68

4) SUM OF THE YEAR—DIGITS METHOD: (REDUCING FRACTION METHOD)

The annual depreciation is found out by multiplying a fraction times the amount to be depreciated (cost minus the salvage value). We determine the fraction for any year by the following formula.

$$\text{Fraction for any year} = \frac{\text{The years of life remaining at the beginning of accounting period}}{\text{The sum of the years of life of the assets}}$$

Fraction for

$$\text{First year} = \frac{10}{1+2+3+4+5+6+7+8+9+10} = \frac{10}{55}$$

$$\text{Second year} = \frac{9}{1+2+3+4+5+6+7+8+9+10} = \frac{9}{55}$$

Just as we compute depreciation by straight line method, similarly we deduct salvage value from original cost each year for finding the annual depreciation:

Rate of annual depreciation = (Original cost – Junk value) × Fraction for the particular year

The value of a tractor is Rs. 92,000 and expected to last for 10 years.

Example: Table 7.3. Sum of the year—Digits Method

Year	Value at the beginning of year	Annual depreciation	Remaining balance
1	92,000	$92000 - 9200 \times \frac{10}{55}$ = Rs 15054 .55	Rs. 92,000 – Rs. 15,054.55 = Rs. 76,945.55
2	76,945.55	$92000 - 9200 \times \frac{9}{55}$ = Rs. 13549 .09	Rs. 76945.55 – Rs. 13549.09 = Rs. 63,396.46
3	63,396.46	$92000 - 9200 \times \frac{8}{55}$ = Rs. 12043 .64	Rs. 63396.46 – Rs. 12,043.64 = Rs. 51,352.82
4	51,352.82	$92,000 - 9,200 \times 7/55 = 10,538.18$	51,352.82 –10,538.18 = 40,814.64
5	40,814.64	$92,000 - 9,200 \times 6/55 = 9,032.73$	40,814.64 –9,032.73 = 31,781.91
6	31,781.91	$92,000 - 9,200 \times 5/55 = 7,527.27$	31,781.91 –7,527.27 = 24,254.64
7	24,254.64	$92,000 - 9,200 \times 4/55 = 6,021.82$	24,254.64 –6,021.82 = 18,232.82
8	18,232.82	$92,000 - 9,200 \times 3/55 = 4,516.36$	18,232.82 –4,516.36 = 13,716.46
9	13,716.46	$92,000 - 9,200 \times 2/55 = 3,010.90$	13,716.46 –3,010.90 = 10,705.56
10	10,705.56	$92,000 - 9,200 \times 1/55 = 1,505.45$	10,705.56 –1,505.45 = 9,200.11

5) COMPOUND INTEREST METHODS

a) Sinking Fund Method

In this system, a depreciation fund equal to the actual loss in the value of the asset or machine is estimated, taking into account, the interest on the so accumulated fund. The rate of depreciation will be constant throughout the life of the machine.

Let D = Rate of depreciation per year
R = Rate of interest on accumulated fund in fraction number
C = Total cost of machine
S = Scrap value
N = No. of years of life of machine

$$D = \frac{R(C - S)}{(1 + R)^N - 1}$$

This will be clear by the following example.

Example 1: A machine is purchased for Rs. 40,000. The estimated life of machine is 15 years and scrap value Rs. 15,000. If the rate of interest on depreciation fund is charged at 5%, calculate the rate of depreciation by sinking fund method.

The required formula is:

$$D = \frac{R(C - S)}{(1 + R)^N - 1}$$

Therefore substituting the values of the example in the formula:

$$D = \frac{0.05 \, (40,000 - 15,000)}{(1 + 0.05)^{15} - 1}$$

$$= \frac{0.05 \times 25,000}{(1.05)^{15} - 1} = \frac{1250}{(2 \cdot 080 - 1)}$$

$$= \frac{1250}{1.08} = \text{Rs. } 1157.40$$

Hence the required amount of depreciation is Rs. 1157.40 per year and this amount is deducted every year for 15 years period.

Example 2: A mechanised farm is having a sugarcane harvest with initial value of Rs. 2,00,000 and the salvage value of Rs. 20,000 at the end of 20 years but is sold for Rs. 1,45,000 at the end of 10 years. What is the profit or loss, if sinking fund depreciation method at 8% compounded annually, was adopted.

Solution:

$$D = \frac{R\,(C-S)}{(1+R)^N - 1}$$

$$= \frac{0.08\,(2,00,000 - 20,000)}{(1+0.08)^{20} - 1}$$

$$= \text{Rs. } 4,342$$

Total amount of depreciation + Interest for 10 years shall be

$$= 9374 + 8680 + 8037 + 7442 + 6800 + 6380 + 5907 + 5570$$
$$+ 5065 + 4689$$
$$= \text{Rs. } 67,934$$

The value of the harvester received at the end of 10 years

$$= 1,45,000 + 67,934 = \text{Rs. } 2,12,934$$

Initial value of the harvester = Rs. 2,00,000

Hence loss to the owner = Rs. 2,12,934 − 2,00,000

$$= \text{Rs. } 12,934$$

b) Annuity Charging Method

In this method, interest is charged on the cost of machine or assets every year on the book value, but the rate of depreciation is constant every year.

Let C = cost of machine

S = scrap value

N = No. of years of machine life

R = Rate of interest in fractions

D = Rate of depreciation

If the value of machine after 1 year becomes C_1, then

$$D = CR + C - C_1 = C\,(1+R) - C_1$$

In the same way, the value of machine after 2 years will be say C_2, then

$$D = C_1 R + C_1 - C_2 = C_1\,(1+R) - C_2$$

Hence the standard formula will be:

$$D = \frac{\{C\,(1+R)^N - S\,\}\,\{1 - (1+R)\}}{1 - (1+R)^N}$$

Example 3: Find the depreciation annuity by the annuity charging method after 3 years, when the cost of pumpset is Rs. 8,000 and scrap value is Rs. 4,000. Rate of interest is 5%.

Solution: By substituting the different values in the above formula the rate of depreciation can be calculated.

$$R = 5\% = 0.05$$
$$C = \text{Rs. } 8,000$$
$$S = \text{Rs. } 4,000$$
$$N = 3 \text{ years}$$

$$D = \frac{\{C\,(1+R)^N - S\,\}\,\{1-(1+R)\}}{1-(1+R)^N}$$

$$= \frac{\{8,000\,(1+0.05)^3 - 4,000\}\,\{1-(1+0.05)\}}{1-(1+0.05)^3}$$

$$= \frac{\{8,000\,(1.05)^3 - 4,000\}\,(1-1.05)}{1-(1.05)^3}$$

$$= \frac{(8,000 \times 1.16 - 4,000)\,(-0.05)}{1-1.16}$$

$$= \frac{5,280 \times 0.05}{0.16} = \text{Rs. } 1,650$$

Hence depreciation annuity = Rs. 1,650

Now, suppose we have to calculate the reduced value of a set after two years. It can be done in this way

$$D = \frac{\{C\,(1+R)^N - S\,\}\,\{1-(1+R)\}}{1-(1+R)^N}$$

Hence now S will become C_2, where C_2 is the reduced value of asset after two years and therefore $N = 2$ years. Hence by substitution:

$$1650 = \frac{8000\,(1+0.05)^2 - C_2\,\{1-(1+0.5)\}}{1-(1+0.05)}$$

$$1650 = \frac{8000 \times 1.1 - C_2\,(-0.05)}{-0.1}$$

$$1650 \times 2 = 8,800 - C_2$$

$$C_2 = 8,800 - 3,300 = \text{Rs.} 5,500$$

∴ The reduced value of asset after two years will be Rs. 5,500 only.

6; THE INSURANCE POLICY METHOD

This method covers the risk, if the machine becomes unserviceable before its estimated life. In this method the machine is insured with the insurance company and premiums are paid on the insurance policy.

When the policy matures, the company provides sufficient sum to replace the machine.

7) MACHINE HOUR BASIS METHOD

In this method, the rate of depreciation is calculated, considering the total number of hours a machine runs in a year, and therefore a work-hour chart of every machine is maintained to know the total number of hours the machine runs in a year.

Example 4: A machine is costing Rs. 11,000 and expected to run for 10 years, at the end of which its scrap value is likely to be Rs. 1000. The machine is expected to run 2000 hours/year on the average. Estimate the depreciation charges per hour of the machine.

Solution:

Cost of machine = Rs. 11,000

Scrap value = Rs. 1,000

Depreciation fund = Rs. 11000–1000 = Rs. 10,000

Life of machine = 10 years = 10 × 2000

$$= 20,000 \text{ hours}$$

Depreciation charges per hour $= \dfrac{10,000}{20,000} = 50$ paise per hour.

Liabilities

The debts or amounts of money owned by an individual, partnership or corporation to others are called liabilities. Liabilities are the commitments of the farmer. This may be in the form of loans, promisory notes, material bought on credit, etc. Liabilities are of three types:

1) Long duration liabilities: These are those which do not require repayment during current accounting period, e.g. long-term loans.

2) Intermediate Liabilities: These can be differed or postponed for the present, but fall due within the year, e.g. promisory notes, medium term and short-term loans.

3) Current liabilities: Repayment of these liabilities may be immediately paid.

Net Worth Statement (Balance Sheet)

The net worth statement shows the financial condition and stability of the business at a particular point of time. Net worth is shown as an excess of assets over liabilities, i.e. the liability of the business to the farmer or farmer's claim in the business.

In summary form, the balance sheet can be illustrated as follows:

Liabilities	Rs. 40,000	Assets	Rs. 60,000
Net capital	Rs. 20,000		
	Rs. 60,000		

On the right hand side are the assets of the business, that is what the business is worth. On the left are the liabilities, that is, what the business owes. The net capital, otherwise known as the capital balance, net worth or equity, is the balancing item. Thus assets (Rs. 60,000) – liabilities (Rs. 40,000) = Net capital (Rs. 20,000).

Net worth or equity is the sum of what would remain to the owner, if the business were sold and all the liabilities paid. If there were a net capital deficit instead of a surplus, this would have to be included on the assets side to balance, and it would mean that the business was insolvent. The details of the asset side of the balance sheet show how the capital is being used in the business, and those on the liabilities side the sources of that capital.

Net worth statement is thus prepared for the farmer and not for his business. It shows whether the business is expanding or shrinking. The business is said to be solvent, when the net worth or equity is greater than zero.

ANALYSIS OF NET WORTH STATEMENT

The net worth calculated above shows only the absolute amounts, by which total assets differ from total liabilities at a point of time. This may not give the true picture of the financial position of the farmer.

1) Net capital ratio
2) Working ratio
3) Current ratio

$$1)\ \text{Net capital ratio} = \frac{\text{Total assets}}{\text{Total liabilities}}$$

It is measured to workout the degree of financial safety over a period of time. Higher the ratio, the safer is the business and the less vulnerable to an unexpected drop in the value of its assets or losses.

$$\frac{1,45,000}{26,000} = 5.6$$

Net worth for two farmers may be the same, but net capital ratio would be different.

$$\text{Farmer (A)}\ \frac{40,000}{30,000} = 1.3 \text{ and Farmer (B) } \frac{20,000}{10,000} = 2.0$$

Business of farmer *B* is in much safer and stable position than that of *A*.

Net worth statement of a farmer as on 1st July, 1986, is as follows:

Liabilities (Rs.)			*Assets* (Rs.)	
1) *Current liabilities*		1) *Current assets*	
Short term loans	--	a) Cash in bank	15,000
Hand loans	2,000	b) Cash on hand	2,000
Fertilisers	2,000	c) A/c receivable	2,000
Feeds	1,000	d) Feed, grain etc.	1,000
Sub-total	5,000	Sub-total	20,000
2) *Intermediate liabilities*		2) *Working assets*	
Loans on machinery and equipment	15,000	Machinery and equipment	25,000
Loans on milch animals	6,000	Livestock	10,000
Sub-total	21,000	Sub-total	35,000
3) *Fixed liabilities*	Nil	3) *Fixed assets*	
		Land	80,000
		Farm buildings	10,000
		Sub-total	90,000
Total of all liabilities	26,000	Total of all assets	1,45,000
Networth	1,19,000		
	1,45,000		1,45,000

Net worth as on 1.7.86 = Total assets – total liabilities
= Rs. 1,45,000 – Rs. 26,000 = Rs. 1,19,000.

2) Working ratio: This measures the financial safety of the business over an intermediate period of time.

$$\text{Working ratio} = \frac{\text{Sum of working and current assets}}{\text{Sum of medium–term liabilities and current liabilities}}$$

$$\frac{55,000}{26,000} = 2 \cdot 1$$

3) Current ratio = $\dfrac{\text{Current assets}}{\text{Current liabilities}}$

It measures the degree of immediate solvency. The aspect of stability described in net capital ratio relates to the long-term solvency of the business. However, the business also has to survive in the shorter run, weathering the temporary stresses and strains that may occur. An important measure in this regard is the current ratio. The higher the ratio, the safer is the firm in the short run, because the more likely it is to survive unexpected demands from creditors.

$$\text{Current ratio} = \frac{20,000}{5,000} = 4.0$$

All these ratios can be compared overtime. Wider these ratios, the better will be the financial position of the business.

Farm Efficiency Measures

An important element in farm business management or decision making relates to the manner in which available resources are allocated. A measuring indicator is necessary to provide guides and standard for appraising accuracy of decisions regarding the use of resources. Efficiency can be related to:

1) The operation of farm business as a whole
2) Any individual phase of the business, line of production or enterprise
3) The use of various factors of production or resources
4) To any single input

Various efficiency measures, therefore need to be developed to express technical efficiency in various farm enterprises and to relate these to the financial success.

The various farm efficiency measures can be discussed as:

1) Physical efficiency measures (technical efficiency)
2) Value efficiency measures (financial efficiency)

They can be further categorised into:

a) Aggregate or absolute measures
b) Ratio measures

1) PHYSICAL EFFICIENCY MEASURES

  a) Aggregate measures
    i) Total area of the farm
    ii) No. of livestock
    iii) Total production

b) Ratio measures
   i) Land use efficiency
      • Yield per acre
      • Production efficiency
      • Crop yield index
      • Intensity of cropping
      • Percentage of land under selected crops
   ii) Labour efficiency
      • Crop acreage/man
      • Productive man—Work-equivalent
   iii) Machinery efficiency
      • Horse power/acre of land available and used

Some of these are explained as follows:

a) Total Area of the Farm

Measuring the acreage of the farm either of total land or land under crops. This is a fairly satisfactory measure for comparing a given type of land and a given type of farming. One can consider the number of standard acres under each situation and compare the size of farms.

b) Land Use Efficiency

Indices of land use efficiency measures the rate of production.

i) Yield per acre = Total production/No. of acres

ii) The production efficiency of a farm with respect to any particular crop enterprise can be expressed in terms of percentage as compared with the average yield of the locality.

Example: Paddy yield per acre of farm (A) = 30 qtls
           Average yield of the locality = 25 qtls

$$\text{Production efficiency of farm } (A) = \frac{30 \times 100}{25} = 120\%$$

iii) Crop yield index is a measure of comparison of the yields of all crops on a given farm, with the average yields of those crops in the locality. The relationship is expressed in percentage terms. This is a convenient measure, because it combines all the yields into a single figure.

iv) Intensity of cropping measures the extent of the use of land for cropping purposes during a given year. It is expressed as percentage.

$$\text{Cropping intensity} = \frac{\text{Area cropped}}{\text{Total cultivated area}} \times 100$$

$$\text{or}$$
$$\frac{\text{Gross cropped area}}{\text{Net area cropped}} \times 100$$

Table 7.4. An example for measurement of crop yield index.

Crop	Average yield, qtls.		Acres of crop on Farm A	Crop yield of farm A as a % age of locality (Col. 3)/ (Col. 2) × 100	% age multiplied by acres
	Locality	Farm A			
Cotton	10	15	2	150	300
Paddy	15	20	8	133	1,064
Maize	20	10	4	50	200
Total			14		1,564

$$\text{Crop yield index} = \frac{1564}{24} = 111.71$$

Examples of cropping intensity

Example 1
Area cropped = 3 acres
Total cultivated Area = 5 acres
Intensity of cropping = $\frac{3}{5} \times 100 = 60\%$

Example 2
Area cropped = 15 acres
Total cultivated area = 10 acres
Intensity of cropping = $\frac{15}{10} \times 100 = 150\%$

2) LABOUR EFFICIENCY MEASURES

a) Crop Acreage Per Man Equivalent
The significance of this measure is influenced by the varying proportion of crops with high or low labour requirements. It is one of the simplest measures and is computed by dividing the total acres in crops by man equivalents.

b) Productive Man-work Units Per Man Equivalent (P.M.W.U./man)
It is another good and accurate general measure of labour efficiency. It is computed by dividing total productive man work units by the number of man equivalents on the farm.

$$P.M.W.U./man = \frac{Total\ P.M.W.U.}{No.\ of\ man\ equivalents}$$

A productive man work unit is the average amount of work accomplished by one man in the usual eight-hour day or 10-hour day. The total P.M.W.U. from a given farm represent the number of 10-hour days or 8-hour days required under average conditions and abilities to do all the work necessary on the crops. The P.M.W.U. are obtained by multiplying the acres of each crop and number of each kind of livestock by the average labour requirements per unit of each enterprise in a region.

P.M.W.U. = Acres of each crop × Average labour requirements
per unit of each crop.

3) FINANCIAL EFFICIENCY MEASURES—AGGREGATE AND RATIO MEASURES

Aggregate measures
i)   Total capital managed
ii)   Gross income
iii) Gross expenses
iv)   Gross profit
v)   Net worth = Total assets − total liabilities

Farm Income and Profit Efficiency Measures
vi)   Net cash income = Total cash receipts − Total cash operating
                                          expenses
vii) Net farm income = Net cash income ± Change in inventory and
                                          depreciation
viii) Farm Earnings = Net farm income + Value of farm privileges
ix)   Family labour earnings = Farm earnings − Interest charges on
                                          farm capital
x)   Returns to Management = Family labour earnings − Imputed
                                          value of family labour
xi)   Percent returns to
      capital $\quad = \dfrac{Farm\ earnings-Family\ labour\ value}{Average\ capital\ investment} \times 100$

Ratio Measures
i)   Gross output per gross input
ii)   Fertiliser cost per crop acres = Fertiliser cost/crop acres
iii) Power and equipment cost per crop acre

$$= \frac{Total\ costs\ of\ machinery}{Total\ crop\ acres}$$

iv) Power and equipment/ Investment per acre

$$= \frac{\text{Total machinery investment}}{\text{Total crop acres}}$$

v) Cost Ratios
- Operating cost ratio $= \dfrac{\text{Operating expenses}}{\text{Gross profit}}$

- Fixed cost ratio $= \dfrac{\text{Fixed expenses}}{\text{Gross profit}}$

- Gross cost ratio $= \dfrac{\text{Total expenses}}{\text{Gross income}}$

- Cost per acre $= \dfrac{\text{Total expenses}}{\text{No. of acres}}$

vi) Capital Ratios
- Capital per unit of gross profit $= \dfrac{\text{Total capital investment}}{\text{Gross income}}$
- Capital per man

vii) Income Ratios
- Rate of capital turnover $= \dfrac{\text{Gross income}}{\text{Total farm assets}} \times 100$

- Net income per acre $= \dfrac{\text{Gross income} - \text{Gross expenses}}{\text{No. of acres}}$

viii) Financial Solvency Ratios
- Net capital ratio
- Working ratio
- Current ratio

Cost ratios: Most of the ratios or efficiency factors indicate strong or weak points in the organisation or operation of the business and to call attention to the specific phase or angles of the business, where greater managerial attention is needed. In addition, there are other ratios which deal with the relationship between costs and returns, relationship of capital investment to income, and the rate of activity or turnover of the capital.

Cost ratios are averages and their magnitudes reflect physical production efficiency, selection of enterprises, prices received for commodities and the expenses for the production elements.

- Operating ratio is the percentage which operating expenses absorb out of gross profit. Improvement in the operating efficiency is directly reflected in this ratio. It may also increase or decrease due to commodity price changes.

 • Fixed ratio can be explained as follows. Fixed expenses continue in about the same amount regardless of the current operating policy. For a growing efficient business, the rate of increase in gross income should be faster than the rate of increase in fixed costs. Little can be done to reduce total fixed costs within a short period, but their magnitude relative to output can be reduced by expanding production.

 • Gross cost ratio is the combined measure of the profit-making ability of the farm and profit margin. Comparison between farms should be made only when the farms are of the same general organisation. Gross ratio expresses the percentage of gross income consumed by expenses and is therefore independent of absolute size of the business.

c) An Example of Measuring the Farm Income and Profit Efficiency

	Item	Farm A (Rs.)	Farm B (Rs.)
i)	Net cash income from		
	• Sale of crops	3000	6000
	• Sale of milk	1000	800
	• Sale of eggs	500	300
	• Miscellaneous sales	200	200
		4700	7300
ii)	Cash expenses		
	• Labour	600	800
	• Seeds	200	200
	• Fertiliser	400	550
	• Purchase of feeds	300	200
	• Miscellaneous	100	250
		1600	2000
iii)	Change in inventory	300	900
iv)	Farm privileges	600	1000
v)	Interest charges on av. farm capital @ 10%	200	375
vi)	Imputed value of family labour	450	800
	• Net cash income (A) = (i – ii)	3100	5300
	• Net farm income (B) = (A +iii)	3400	6200
	• Farm earnings (D) = (B + iv)	4000	7200
	• Family labour earnings (E) = (D – v)	3800	6825
	• Returns to management (F) = (E – vi)	3350	6025

Capital ratios: Rate of capital turnover is the most common measure of capital efficiency. It is the ratio of the total farm income to the farm capital (total farm assets). The rate of capital turnover indicates the number of years required for the farm receipts (income) to equal the average farm capital. A faster turnover rate is a sign of good farm business. A high rate of turnover is especially important for the beginning farmer, who is short of capital. This rate ordinarily varies widely with the type of farm investments.

4) FARM COSTING

Cost refers to the money value of effort expended or sacrifice made in producing an article or rendering a service or achieving a specific purpose.

Economists have developed different cost concepts and new ideas which are more relevant to planning and control of business activities. The overall objective is achieving cost efficiency through appropriate techniques of cost control and cost reduction. As such, almost all forms of business decisions centre on cost, so the cost efficiency could be a reality.

a) Role of Costs in Farm Management

i) It helps in choosing from among varied alternative courses of action.

ii) It helps in pricing decisions.

iii) Cost helps in determining the optimum level of operation in accordance with the behaviour of cost in relation to scale of operation.

iv) In deciding replacement of a capital equipment by a new one, cost information is vital.

v) In deciding whether to sell a product at one stage of processing or to further process it, cost data are needed.

vi) In deciding the acquisition of fixed assets, again cost is a relevant factor.

vii) To decide whether an equipment is to be bought or hired cost data are essential.

viii) Lastly, cost plays a vital role in performance evaluation and returns analysis.

There are different cost concepts but all are not relevant in all decisions.

b) Opportunity Cost versus Actual Cost

Opportunity cost refers to the value of benefits of a foregone alternative. Simply it means the income from the missed alternative. It follows that opportunity cost would arise only when there are alternatives. It is specially used in resource allocation problems, when the resource in question can be put to plural uses, but one at a time.

c) Out-of-pocket versus Imputed Cost

Out-of-pocket cost refers to cost that involves an actual outlay of cash immediately, or in the near future. Material cost, labour cost and interest on borrowed funds are examples of out-of-pocket cost. On the other hand, imputed cost does not involve actual outlay. It refers to assumed costs or hypothetical costs. It includes the assumed costs of using owned resources for the business carried on by the farm owner himself. Assumed interest on owned capital, assumed remuneration for owner's service or family labour contribution, assumed rental charges on owned land, are some typical examples. For decision making, the imputed cost is irrelevant, as it does not affect the business funds and the cost of operation of the farm business. On the other hand, cost involving actual outlay is relevant as the farm manager can plan it and exercise control over it.

d) Cost Concepts

The cost concepts approach to farm costing is widely used in India. These cost concepts, in brief, are Cost-A_1; Cost-A_2; Cost-B and Cost-C. The different cost items that are to be included under each cost concept are detailed below with their imputational procedures and examples.

Cost-A_1: It includes the value of:
- Casual hired labour
- Attached labour
- Hired bullock labour
- Imputed value of owned bullock labour
- Hired machine labour
- Imputed value of owned machine labour
- Seeds
- Manures and fertilisers
- Plant protection chemicals
- Irrigation charges
- Interest on working capital
- Depreciation
- Land revenue
- The total of all these cost items make up Cost-A_1.

Cost A_2 : Cost A_1 + rent paid for leased-in land, if any.

Cost-B: Cost A$_2$ + imputed rental value of owned land + Interest on owned fixed capital.

Cost -C: Cost B + imputed value of family labour. Cost-C is the total cost of cultivation or gross cost.

5) IMPUTATION PROCEDURES AND GUIDELINES TO BE FOLLOWED WHILE ESTIMATING COST OF CULTIVATION OF CROPS

a) Casual Labour: Actual cash wages or kind wages and perquisites are to be imputed, considering the ruling prices in the village at the time of operations.

b) Attached servants: The per day wage rate is to be arrived at, based on total wages (Cash + Kind + Perquisites) paid and the number of days.

c) Bullock labour: Hired—actual charges paid are considered. In case of owned bullock labour—per work day or per work hour cost of maintenance is to be taken into account.

d) Cost of maintenance/year:
    i) Cost towards feeds and fodder
    ii) Concentrates
    iii) Veterinary charges
    iv) Upkeep (men proportionate charges)
    v) Depreciation and interest charges on the value of cattle shed
    vi) Other charges
Total costs per year (i to vi)
Total Receipts, from (a) hiring out in a year, (b) value of FYM and (c) others.
Net maintenance charges per year = Total costs – total receipts
Number of work days or hours per year
Cost of maintenance per work day or work hour

$$\text{(or Bullock pair day/hour)} \quad = \frac{\text{Net maintenance cost per year}}{\text{Number of work days in a year}}$$

e) Owned manures, seeds and others are to be imputed at the prices prevailing in the village at the time of their use.

f) Interest on working capital—Interest on entire cash costs are to be charged at $11\frac{1}{2}$ per cent for half of the crop period. Actual interest charges are to be considered in respect of borrowed capital.

g) Depreciation on fixed assets (other than the value of land) such as farm implements, farm buildings, irrigation structures, work cattle, pumpsheds, following the straight line method.

h) Rent on owned land—30 per cent of the output (main product plus by-product) is to be considered as rental value of owned land or existing rental values in the village.

i) Interest on owned fixed capital (other than the land value). It is to be charged at 10 per cent.

j) Family labour—Men family labour is to be charged on par with the attached servants (average) of the village, while family women labour is to be imputed considering the wages paid to the women labour for similar operations.

Table 7.5. Break up of cost of cultivation in Rupees—Crop-wise

(Rupees/hectare)

Inputs	Crops					
	Paddy		Sugarcane		Turmeric	
	Cost	Percent	Cost	Percent	Cost	Percent
Cost A₁:						
Casual Labour	565.00	9.97	2,150.00	16.86	2,000.00	12.44
Attached labour	120.00	2.12	300.00	2.35	600.00	3.73
Bullock labour						
Hired	30.00	0.53	50.00	0.39	60.00	0.37
Owned	—	—	—	—	—	—
Machine labour:						
Owned	—	—	—	—	—	—
Hired	450.00	7.94	1,500.00	11.76	100.00	0.62
Seeds	30.00	0.53	1,000.00	7.84	3,000.00	18.66
Manures & fertilisers	500.00	8.82	1,000.00	7.84	700.00	4.35
Insecticides	200.00	3.53	550.00	4.31	400.00	2.49
Irrigation	112.00	1.98	174.30	1.37	200.00	1.24
Interest on working capital	40.71	0.72	316.25	2.48	414.28	2.58
Depreciation	845.48	14.92	679.30	5.33	757.90	4.71
Land Revenue	50.00	0.88	50.00	0.39	50.00	0.31
Total of Cost A₁:	2,943.19	51.93	7,770.65	60.93	8,282.18	51.52
Rent or paid for leased in land	—	—	—	—	—	—
Total of Cost A₂:	2,943.19		7,770.65		8,282.18	31.72
Rent on owned land	1,020.00	18.00	3,345.30	26.23	5,100.00	7.40
Interest on owned fixed capital	1,189.00	20.98	778.09	6.10	1189.00	—
Total of Cost B:	5,152.19	90.91	11,894.04	93.26	14,571.15	90.63
Family labour wages	515.29	9.09	860.00	6.74	1,505.64	9.37
Total of Cost C: (Total costs)	5,667.40	100.00	12,754.04	100.00	16,076.82	100.00

k) The actual costs plus transport charges are to be considered in case of other purchased inputs, such as fertilisers, insecticides, etc.

l) Machine labour—Actual hire charges are to be taken and in case of owned machine, prevailing hire charges are to be adopted.

After imputation, the proportionate charges (based on gross cropped area and total costs per farm) of each item is to be considered in the costs of crops, for which these inputs are used in the farm. An example worked out on the above guidelines is presented in table 7.5.

6) RATES OF RETURN OVER DIFFERENT COST CONCEPTS

a) Gross returns—Value of main product plus by-product. The main products and by-products are to be imputed taking into account the actual marketed prices, otherwise the village level prices prevailing at the time of enquiry.

The following measures of returns over different concepts are measured and shown in table 7.6.

b) Farm business income = Gross income − Cost-A_1
c) Family labour income = Gross income − Cost-B
d) Net income =. Gross income − Cost-C
e) Farm investment income= Farm business income − Wages of family labour.

Work out cost of production at Cost-A_1, Cost-B and Cost-C level per (quintal) unit of output, by dividing the net costs (gross costs minus value of by-product) by the output.

Dr. Sen's special expert committee for improving the cost of cultivation/production estimates (1979) recommended the following classification of costs to be adopted:

Cost-A_1: All actual expenses in cash and kind incurred in production by owner operator.

Cost-A_2: Cost-A_1 + rent paid for leased-in land.

Cost-B_1: Cost-A_1 + interest on value of owned capital assets (excluding land).

Cost-B_2: Cost-B_1 + rental value of owned land (net of the land revenue) and rent paid for leased-in land.

Cost-C_1: Cost B_1 + imputed value of family labour.
Cost-C_2: Cost-B_2 + imputed value of family labour.

Including managerial or supervisor cost as part of cost of production. In Indian agriculture, normally the farmer combines in himself both the functions of operation and management, which are very difficult to separate out in practice. The Sen's committee felt that the time disposi-

tion (in arranging supplies of inputs, etc.) and actual expenses on supervision or managerial function on the whole farm can be estimated.
Evaluating the time spent at the family labour rate and adding the actual
expenses will appropriate the total expenses on managerial functions.

Table 7.6. Rates of return over different cost components (Rs./ha)

S. No.	Item	Paddy	Sugarcane	Turmeric
1.	Gross returns	8,608.00	11,343.56	17,000
	Value of main product	8,208.00	11,000.00	17,000
.	Value of by-product	400.00	343.56	
2.	Farm Business income	5,664.81	3,572.91	8,717.82
	(Gross income — Cost-A$_1$)			
3.	Family labour income	3,455.81	−550.48	2,428.82
	(Gross income—Cost-B)			
4.	Net income	2,940.60	−1410.48	923.18
	(Gross income—Cost-C)			
5.	Farm investment income	5,149.60	2,712.91	7,212.18
	(Farm business income — Family labour wages)			
Cost of Production				
1.	Net cost	5,267.40	12,410.48	16,076.82
	(Gross cost—value of by-product)			
2.	Output/ha (qtls)	45.60	820.00	45.00
3.	Cost of production per quintal of output	115.51	15.13	357.26

6) TREATMENT OF TRANSPORTATION COSTS

The question, whether transportation is part of cost of production/
cultivation or not is sometimes raised. Since the producer participates in
the selling process, the expenses incurred by him on this account should
be considered to belong to the production process itself, and therefore is
included in the cost of production.

CHAPTER 8

Farm Planning and Budgeting

Planning is the deliberate and conscious effort on the part of the farmer to think about the farm programmes in advance and adjust them according to new knowledge on technological developments, changes in physical and economic situations, price structures, etc.

Scientific planning is systematic and written based on the best information available and aimed at achieving the maximum of satisfaction for the farmer and his family out of their resources.

What is Farm Planning?

Farm planning implies the adoption of business method in every phase of farm activity. It is a decision making process. Farm planning approach is an integrated, co-ordinated and advance programme of actions, which seek to present an opportunity to cultivators to improve his level of income.

Farm planning is an approach which introduces desirable changes in farm organisation and operations and makes the farm a viable unit. Farm planning is a process of making decisions regarding the organisation and operation of a farm business, so that it results in a continuous maximisation of net returns of a farm business.

Why Farm Planning?

On majority of our farms, there is under-utilisation as well as over-utilisation of the existing farm resources. Due to this our farmers fail to get optimum and maximum net gains. There is immediate necessity to re-organise the farm structure and for proper allocation of resources to obtain maximum net income and optimum production. This calls for proper farm planning and budgeting.

The main objective of farm planning is to maximise net income and it involves "Planning Horizon". The length of the planning period on the basis of the farmers situation has to be therefore decided. The main objective, is to maximise the annual net income sustained over a long period of time.

Types of Farm Planning
1) Simple farm planning
2) Complete or full farm planning

1) Simple farm planning is adopted either for a part of land, for one enterprise, or to substitute one resource by another. This is very simple and easy to understand as well as to implement. The process of change should always begin with the simple farm planning.

2) Complete farm planning envisages farm planning for the whole farm, i.e. for all enterprises on the farm, for a change in the farm structure and organisation. Complete farm planning aims for a complete change in cropping programme, more towards specialised farming, more income and market orientation.

Essential Elements of Farm Planning
Economic planning involves the manipulation of limited resources among alternative opportunities, in order to satisfy the set objective of maximising profit. It follows that any planning procedure must contain three essential elements:

(1) an objective, (2) scarce resources and (3) the enterprises for using the resources to attain the objective (alternative ways).

The main aim or objective in planning the allocation of resources is to maximise profit. However, farmers commonly have other objectives as well, which must be taken into account in practical planning. In any form of planning, the principle of profit-maximisation cannot be abandoned. The resources available to the farmer act as a framework, within which he must plan his farm activities. The concern is with those resources that are relatively scarce, although it is frequently impossible to decide in advance which resources will prove to be limiting, so that it becomes part of the planning process, to detect them. The resources available to the farmer distinguish the feasible from the unfeasible enterprises. Fixed resources place a limit on the maximum level of production; from individual enterprises fixed resources influence the level of input, both of other fixed resources and of variable resources. The limitations of resources determine the most suitable organisation to be added within individual enterprises.

The enterprises are the third element, representing alternative ways of using the fixed resources in seeking to attain the objective. The information that is required about the enterprises before planning are:
1) Financial returns
2) Requirements of variable inputs
3) Requirements of fixed resources

Without information on the financial returns to be expected in the enterprises, it would be impossible to attain the set objective of maximising net income, because there would be no criterion on which to base their selection. Variable inputs are items such as, fertilisers, feed stuffs, etc., the use of which alters in direct proportion to changes in the balance of individual enterprises, within a given framework of fixed resources. Many factors affect the level of variable inputs. They include the quality of fixed resources, the intensity of production, the methods adopted and the efficiency with which they are applied. The financial returns and the variable costs have one feature in common, namely they both vary together with changes in the size of enterprises. Deducting the variable costs from the output of an enterprise leaves the gross margin and it is the latter that becomes the guide, as to which enterprises to select in seeking to maximise net income. The fixed resources available at any particular point of time constitute a planning framework; the unit requirements of fixed resources vary with the production methods adopt and the relative efficiency with which they are applied. It is possible to raise the limits imposed on an enterprise, both by lowering fixed resource requirements and by acquiring more fixed resources. Knowledge of fixed resource requirements is also needed to enable the return (gross margin) to the resources used in different enterprises to be calculated.

Stages of Farm Planning

Stage 1 : Adoption of package of practices (selected enterprises) — envisages no change in the cropping pattern.

Stage 2 : Extension of stage 1 to all crop enterprises on the farm. Here also no major change is envisaged. The farmer has to use all the recommended practices on all the major enterprises simultaneously.

Stage 3: Final stage full farm plan. Major change is envisaged in farm structure and organisation. It requires considerable training in farm management. Detailed farm plans are to be prepared to get maximum income from resources.

Principal Characteristics of a Good Farm Plan

1) It should provide for efficient use of farm resources, such as labour, power and equipment.

2) The crop plan should have balanced combination of enterprises, i.e. it should do the following:

a) Provide for given minimum production of different food, cash and fodder crops.

b) Help to maintain and improve soil fertility.

c) Help to raise and stabilise farm earnings

d) Improve distribution and use of labour, power and water requirements throughout the year

e) Avoid excessive risks

f) Provide flexibility

g) Utilise, the farmers knowledge, training, experience and take into account of the farmers likes and dislikes

h) Give considerations to efficient marketing facilities

i) Provide programme of obtaining, using and repaying the credit

j) Provide for all of up-to-date modern agricultural methods and practices.

Basic Steps of Farm Planning and Budgeting

1) Assessment of resources—survey of actual conditions of the farm and the availability of resources and use

2) Analysis of the existing plan operations

3) Identification of the problems, detection of loop-holes and defects of the present plans

4) Discussion with the farmers and other specialists to examine the possibilities for improvement through alternative plan operations

5) Preparation of alternative plans on the basis of existing co-efficients and discussion with the farmer

6) Selection of final plan for implementation

Farm Budgeting

The budget is essentially a presentation of costs and returns, accompanied by a statement showing the physical quantities of inputs and output associated with each value figure. The objective of drawing up a budget is to measure the returns expected from the plan.

Farm budgeting is a method of analysing plans for the use of agricultural resources at the command of the decision maker. A farm plan is a programme of the total farm activity of a farmer drawn up in advance. The expression of a farm plan in monetary terms by estimation of receipts, expenses and net income is called budgeting.

In other words, farm budgeting is a process of estimating costs, returns and net profit of a farm or a particular enterprise. Planning and budgeting go side by side.

The three common objectives of farm budgeting are:

1) To estimate the profitability of a particular pattern of organisation

2) To determine the change in profits that are likely to follow a particular change in organisation
3) To compare different organisational patterns or alternative changes in organisation on a profit basis

Types of Farm Budgeting

There are two ways of presenting a budget.
1) Partial budgeting (Enterprise budgeting)
2) Complete budgeting (Full budgeting)

1) PARTIAL BUDGETING

It refers to estimating the outcome or returns for a part of the business, i.e. one or a few activities. In situations, where relatively small modifications have to be made to the existing organisation, a partial budget will suffice.

The partial budget is conveniently presented in the form of an account, with the source of increased revenue and added costs associated with the proposed change in organisation on the *credit side*, and the details of increase in costs and reduction in revenue on the *debit side*. The extra profit or loss likely to arise out of the proposed plan, is then derived from the difference between the two totals.

2) COMPLETE BUDGETING

This method is used to make out a plan for the whole farm. In situations involving extensive remodelling of the farm organisation, a full budget is called for. This entails setting out all the individual cost and return items for the farm, so that the overall net return is from the whole unit. It relates to efforts to consider all aspects of farm organisation simultaneously. In preparing the complete budget, all the physical data are included and all cost and receipt items have to be calculated. This procedure includes six main steps.
a) Listing available resources and stating objectives
b) Estimating crop areas and livestock numbers
c) Estimating physical inputs and outputs
d) Estimating factor and product prices; calculating costs and returns
e) Estimating fixed costs
f) Totals and layout of budget

How to Work out a Partial Budget?

In working out partial budgets, we need to know about four important elements. Four questions are asked in a partial budget, two of which relate to the financial losses arising from the contemplated change (i.c. the debit side) and two of which relate to the consequential financial gains (i.e. credit side).

a) Debits: What loss of present revenue occurs? What extra new costs are incurred?

b) Credits: What extra new revenue is obtained? What present costs are no longer incurred?

ELEMENTS OF PARTIAL BUDGETING
   a) Added costs
   b) Added returns
   c) Reduced costs
   d) Reduced returns

(Total of added returns + reduced costs) – (total of added costs + reduced returns) = Net income from the change made in the farm organisation by partial budgeting.

a) Added costs: These are the costs additionally incurred towards the adjustment made in the operations. Here, only paid out costs are considered.

b) Added returns: These are the returns that are added as result of substitution or adjustment made.

c) Reduced costs: These are the costs, which are incurred due to the particular operation, for which another operation in substituted.

d) Reduced returns: These are the returns which are foregone due to the operation of a particular activity, for which another activity is substituted.

PARTIAL BUDGET

Table 8.1. Adjustment: Soil versus foliar application of nitrogen on paddy crop

Debit	Rs.	Credit	Rs.
(a) Increase in costs per acre		(a) Decrease in costs per acre	
i) Cost of spraying	20.00	i) Fertiliser cost of 10 kg urea @ Rs. 210 qtl.	21.00
ii) Threshing & winnowing cost for 1 qtl.	5.00		
(b) Decrease in returns per acre	—	(b) Increase in returns per acre	
		i) Paddy yield 1 qtl. @ Rs. 150/qtl.	150.00
		ii) Straw of paddy @ 1/kg	10.00
(1) Total of (a) & (b)	25.00	(2) Total of (a) & (b)	181.00

Net gain [change in income: (1)–(2)] = Rs. 181–25 = Rs. 156.00

This partial budget analysis (Table 8.1) shows that the foliar application increases net returns per acre by Rs. 156.00 over soil application.

AN ILLUSTRATION OF FARM PLANNING AND BUDGETING

The success in any plan mainly depends on the systematic procedure followed, which must be easily adoptable and feasible. For easy understanding and practice, an example of alternate farm plans and budgeting techniques prepared is given below:

1) Evaluating the Present Farm Situation

a) RESOURCE POSITION

i) Land

The holding of the farmer is about 5.3 ha. The entire land is wetland with well and completely assured irrigation facilities and adopted to monoculture of paddy by growing the same in both *Kharif* and *Rabi*. In between the fragments of the field a feeding channel of irrigation is there, which is a sub-channel from the irrigation canal nearby.

Type of soil: The soils are black clay type, with higher water holding capacity. It provides poor aeration and highly ill-drained conditions make the soil more problematic. Soil is highly fertile, as there is medium to high ranges in potassium and low to medium in phosphorus and low to medium in nitrogen. It is medium in status of organic matter.

Available nitrogen   :   300 kg/ha
Available P_2O_5 :   30 kg/ha
Available K_2O :   600 kg/ha
pH of soil   :   7.2 to 7.5

Drainage: The soils are not bestowed with good drainage facilities. As by nature the soils are deprived of good drainage, the farmer has not so far adopted any drainage management practices.

Topography: Topography of the land can be deemed as plane. The field has not had any undulations. The fields have a little slope towards drainage canal, of western direction. It helps in draining water into the drain to some extent.

Soil conservation & Water Management: The farmer had not adopted any soil conservation and water management practices. Actually there is no need to undertake either soil or water management practices, since the soils are sticky and hard to get or eroded and adequate water supply throughout the year, except two months in summer. The holes of rats formed in the bunds allows the irrigation water from one field to field. But the farmer does not bother about this leakage of water as there is no scarcity of water.

ii) Labour

Extent of family labour: The ryot is only the person who looks after the farming and the wife is meant for household work and children are being sent to school. So the ryot is a mere supervisor of farm operations and not a labourer.

Permanent labour: The farmer engaged one labourer as permanent, who looks after both the farming operations and tending cattle. For the permanent mazdoor employed, the farmer pays 15 quintals of paddy per annum with a pair of clothes. So, it costs nearly Rs. 2200 per annum.

Labour availability: Labour availability in the village is in surplus. Hence generally scarcity is less. Totally there are 1620 agricultural labourers. All these are not provided the employment in agricultural operations entirely during the days of crop growth and harvest . So some of them will migrate to other areas and some employed for non-agricultural works.

Wages: The wage rates are flexible and vary according to the demand, especially during peak periods like harvesting, weeding, transplanting, etc. But it ranges from Rs. 10 to Rs. 12 per day for men labourer and Rs.8 to Rs.10 per day for women labourer. However, the wage rates may vacillate in either directions.

Peak periods: Peak periods in paddy cultivation are transplanting, weeding and harvesting. Eventhough the labour is in surplus, the demand increases sometimes in peak periods, due to the coincidence of the operation of all the villagers in the surrounding villages on the same days.

iii) Cattle and Mechanical Power Availability

The farmer is having no bullocks or any draught animals. He has only two she buffaloes for obtaining milk and milk products for home consumption. Each buffalo yields milk at 3 litres per day.

Dead stock available: The farmer is having six spades, two crow bars, two wooden planks and a sprayer of knapsack type. They are generally used by the permanent labour and seldom by casual labour, if they are small in number.

Since he has no bullocks or any draught animals, he ploughs and puddles the land with hired tractor. For this operation the hire charges are Rs. 86 per acre. For 13 acres the cost is Rs. 1218. Two hired labour is engaged for lands repair and their shaping.

iv) Capital

Capital required for cultivation of paddy could be managed by the net income that was available from the previous season crop. Sometimes if and when he has no capital, he borrows money from his brothers free of interest and gets cleared when he gets the returns.

v) Organisation

With respect to paddy cultivation, the farmer is skillful, as he is a graduate and has very good interest in agriculture. Still he needs more knowledge as he is less experienced person in agriculture. The extent of knowledge regarding cultivation of paddy is good.

vi) Irrigation

Source: Vijjeswaram Main Canal of Godavari Western Delta.

Coverage: Entire area is covered.

Period of availability: Available throughout the year except summer months, i.e. April and May. Hence for both *Kharif* and *Rabi* seasons there would be no scarcity or shortage of irrigation water.

vii) Other Information

Farm Buildings: There is no farm building for storage, but there is a permanent cattle shed which has been built in 1981 and cost at the time of construction is Rs. 8,000. It is a building with brick walls and thatched roof and without cement flooring. The expected life is seven years.

Equipment & Machinery: The farmer has no equipment or machinery except two wooden planks and knap-sack sprayer. Since the operations of precultivation are generally being done by hired tractors, no need to have any equipment. The two home made wooden planks costing of Rs. 25 each are used for levelling the fields.

A sprayer of knapsack type is generally used for spraying operations. This has been bought in 1977 at the cost of Rs. 450.

b) Crops Grown

The holding of the farmer is 5.3 ha, which is entirely wetland and under paddy cultivation. Monoculture of rice has been the practice (Tables 8.2 and 8.3).

Table 8.2. Levels of production

Crop	Year	Season	Variety	Yield q/ha
Paddy	1984-85	*Kharif*	MTU-7029	49.61
		Rabi	BPT 1235	53.29
Paddy	1985-86	*Kharif*	MTU-7029	44.10
		Rabi	BPT 1235	47.78
Paddy	1986-87	*Kharif*	MTU-2077	49.61
		Rabi	BPT 1235	64.31

Table 8.3. Costs and returns in existing plan

Sl. No.	Crop	Main product (qtls)	By-product (tonnes)	Cost (Rs.)	Main product value (Rs.)	By-product value (Rs.)	Total net returns
1.	Paddy (*Kharif*)	214.50	13	18.200	28,600	1,300	11,700
2.	Paddy (*Rabi*)	263.25	17	19,500	35,100	1,700	17,300

2) Risks in the Farm Production

a) The farmer faces many obstacles in the way for successfully carrying forward the farming enterprise. He must have a risk bearing ability and the strength to withstand the hazards caused by nature. Nature plays with the farmer by creating floods, cyclones with gale winds and other natural calamities.

b) In this region, brown plant hopper has become a great problem and the farmer has to carefully manage with the pest. For the first time in this region, sheath blight has been noticed since two years, which had become very serious on almost all varieties. It has no effective control method, but one can prevent the spread of the disease.

c) Lack of sufficient time, leading to the unattentiveness of the farmer to select the best input combinations for an effective enterprise.

d) Recently, after last year flood havoc of river Godavari, rat caused damage has become a very serious threat to rice crop. Now this menace has become a nightmare to the farmers. During the current season, the rats caused severe damage in the village, to the extent of 10% of the area.

e) In this region, in general the harvesting season coincides with the rains of both monsoons and cyclones. It results in deterioration of the quality of seed. In some varieties the seed germinates due to non-dormancy character.

f) Adequate and excessive supply of irrigation water during *Kharif* season makes the soil poorly aerated and ill drained. These problems get escalated since the soil is black clayey.

g) This district is flood prone, mainly during *Kharif;* when excessive rains are experienced, the Godavari river water flood the fields. It results in severe and some times entire loss of crop, as the water stands on the harvested crop and the crop gets completely damaged.

These are the problematic risks which have been generally facing the farmers in the area, the result of both natural vagaries and, pests and diseases.

3) Weak Points in the Existing Plan

The package of practices that are being followed in the existing plan have been thoroughly analysed to focuss the weakness of the existing plan and remedies for them.

a) The first and foremost point to be considered is monoculture of paddy throughout the year, as both in *Kharif* and *Rabi*. It results in continuous multiplication of pests like BPH and diseases like blast and sheath blight, which have become uncontrollable.

So *Kharif* paddy should be alternated with the pulse or legume crops, like blackgram in *Rabi* season helps in increasing soil fertility, nitrogen addition to soil, and reduce the pest and disease menace.

It can be obvious that crop rotation should be followed.

b) No seed treatment has been practiced for paddy seed. Seed treatment with Bavistin 0.1% or Captan or Thiram 0.3% helps in reducing pest menace.

c) The former almost never applied any phosphatic fertilisers. Some times he applied nitrogenous fertilisers.

d) Correct spacing that is recommended is not being practiced. 33 hills/sq. m in *Kharif* and 44 hills/sq. m in *Rabi* are optimum.

e) As the soil is black clayey, puddling operations taken by the tractor creates deep pits in the corners and also increases the depth of puddling. While transplanting, the labourers plants the seedlings to the deeper layers. It results in death of hills, or slow or no recovery after transplanting.

It requires no capital, except the organisation of the farmer who should supervise the operation to plant in shallow depths to increase the yields.

f) Without the regard of pest, the farmer has been applying only BHC 10%. It is the common practice in the entire area of this region. It results in death of parasites and predators and also has long residual effect.

g) Rats should be controlled collectively, otherwise for one individual it is impossible to control them.

h) The farmer has not taken any drainage management practices.

Some of the above loopholes require mere change of practices by applying new scientific knowledge without the necessity of any capital, to increase the yield.

4) Alternate Farm Plan

For paddy (*Kharif*), the suggestions given for improving the package of practices are as follows:

First of all he should change the crop sequence, and crop rotation should be followed by rotating the *Kharif* paddy with a pulse crop like blackgram in *Rabi* season to get advantages of crop rotation.

Advantages of crop rotation: Crop rotation has the following advantages.

a) Increases the soil fertility by improving the soil texture and structure.

b) Adds nitrogen to the soil as the pulse crop stores nitrogen in their nodules.

c) Reduces the pest prevalence, since there is a break—one season in host life-cycle.

d) Increases the yields of *Kharif* paddy crop.

e) Seed treatment should be followed at the rate of 3 gm of Captan or 1 gm of Bavistin per kg of seed. It would reduce the pest and disease incidence and it will also increase the germination percentage.

f) Phosphatic fertiliser should also be applied to improve the grain quality and to strengthen the plants to stand against pests and diseases. 30 kg of P_2O_5 per ha is required to be applied.

g) Correct spacing should be followed as of 33 hills/sq.m in *Kharif*, to get higher yields.

h) The transplantation should be done at shallow depth and at four to six leaf stage, to early recovery of seedlings and higher yields.

i) Alleys should be prepared at every two metre distance, when transplanting is taken up.

j) The nitrogen fertilisers should be applied in three splits. The entire phosphatic fertiliser and one-third of N as basal (no K_2O application since it is high) and one-third of N at maximum tillering stage and one third of N at panicle initiation stage.

k) The spray fluid of the pesticides like Monochrotophos should be sprayed at recommended doses, and while spraying the nozzle should be diverted to the bases of the hills as the BPH are occurring there.

l) Rats should be controlled collectively.

m) The farmer gets convinced to follow drainage practices by preparing trenches below the field.

As per alternative plan that has been prepared, the main changes chosen to suggest to the farmer in the crop enterprise are:

a) The *Kharif* paddy crop should be taken up with good management practices as listed above.

b) Instead of growing *Rabi* paddy crop, the legume pulse crop is recommended to rotate the crop.

c) Suggested to grow green manure crop during the summer (April to May), i.e. pillipesara and sunhemp. The former one can also be used as fodder crop if required.

These are the suggestions which have been interpreted in the alternative farm plans.

ALTERNATE FARM PLAN-1: Alternate Farm Plan-1 is presented in Table 8.4.

Table 8.4. Analysis of the alternate plan of paddy (*Kharif*) to check the profitability through the use of partial budget technique—cost of cultivation of paddy (*Kharif*)

S.No	Operation	Qty.	Amount	Labour		Wages (Rs.)		Total
				M	W	M	W	amount
1.	Land preparation	—	—	2	1	24	10	110.00
2.	Nursery raising	—	—	2	1	24	10	34.00
3.	F Y M	6 t	111	2	—	24	—	135.00
4.	Seed	25 kg	100	2	—	24	—	124.00
5.	Weeding	—	—	6	11	72	110	182.00
6.	Fertilisers: Urea	75 kg	168	2	—	24	—	244.00
	SSP	50 kg	52					
7.	Irrigation charges	—	—	—	—	—	—	100.00
8.	Harvesting	—	—	2	13	24	130	154.00
9.	Plant protection:							
	Monocrotophos	100ml	80					
	Endosulfan	150ml	80	2	—	24	—	184.00
10.	Land revenue	—	—	—	—	—	—	45.00
11.	Interest charges	—	—	—	—	—	—	159.00
12.	Others, if any:							
	Seed treatment	39kg	35	2	—	24	—	59.00
	Drying	—	—	2	—	24	—	24.00
	Threshing	—	—	2	2	24	20	44.00
				Grand total				1598.00

a) Added costs:

i)	Application of FYM (additional)	Rs. 30.00
ii)	Application of fertilisers	Rs. 50.00
iii)	Application of pesticides	Rs. 40.00
iv)	Additional interest charges on working capital	Rs. 19.00
v)	Seed treatment	Rs. 59.00

Rs. 198.00

b) Reduced cost: Nil

c) Added returns:

Paddy grain yield increases by 450 kg, i.e.

(Rate: Rs. 100 per 75 kg bag) = Rs. 600

d) Reduced returns: Nil

e) Profitability of alternate plan

(Added returns + Reduced cost) − (Reduced returns + Added cost)

= (600.00 + Nil) − (Nil + 198.00)

= 600.00 − 198.00 = Rs. 402.00

f) Cost benefit ratio:

Additional cost = Additional returns

198 : 600

1   : 3.03

That is, for every one rupee additional investment towards following the suggested package of practices, the farmer gets an additional returns of Rs. 3.03.

After the plan was prepared, it was analysed as shown above to know the feasibility of the plan on the farmer's field by convincing him to adopt the suggested plan.

The recommended practices are mainly seed treatment, correct dose of fertilisers at right time, and effective control of pests and diseases. These are the methods which involves capital.

The seed treatment with Captan at the rate of 3 gm/kg of seed (or) and Bavistin, at the rate of 1gm/kg of seed was intended to prevent the seed from seed borne pest and disease, it will prevent their attack up to 35–40 days. Hence this practice has been recommended.

The farmer had been applying higher dosages of N fertilisers without balancing with P fertilisers, which resulted in severe susceptibility of crop to pests and diseases. So the recommended schedule of N and P fertilisers and their time of application were given to the farmer as suggested in alternate plan.

Indiscriminate use of BHC 10% has to be avoided and replaced with sprayings of monocrotophos and other pesticides against BPH. It costs additional Rs. 40.

THE PRACTICES WHICH DO NOT INVOLVE ANY CAPITAL

1) Correct spacing to be adopted
2) Optimum shallow depth of planting
3) Alleys preparation
4) Growing the crop under strict supervision of ryot to identify the pest or disease menace at the initial stage
5) Correct time of application of fertilisers.

PRACTICABILITY OF THE ALTERNATE PLAN

There are no impracticable or hard to practice conditions present in the suggested farm plan. It is feasible to the ryot at his limited conditions.

The cost of cultivation of paddy during *Kharif* season increased by Rs. 198 per 0.40 ha. For this additional cost incurred, the additional benefit of Rs. 600 per acre can be received. The total additional returns for 5.30 ha is Rs. 7,800 for the additional cost of Rs. 2,574.

Most of the suggested package of practices involved no capital, except a few like additional pesticides, fertilisers and seed treatment. So there is no problem regarding capital requirement. There is no complicated techniques or skills required to follow the practices. Since he is a large farmer, he can meet the additional cost from the same resources.

Instead of growing paddy as *Rabi* crop, it been suggested to grow the pulse crop blackgram, to get the following advantages:

1) Higher returns of blackgram over *Rabi* paddy with minimum of risks
2) Improves the soil texture and structure.
3) Supplies highly nutritive fodder.
4) Adds organic matter to the soil.
5) Increases the nitrogen content in soil as the crop has the ability of symbiosis with the nitrogen fixing bacteria and to store nitrogen in its root nodules, which are deposited in the soil.
6) Effective utilisation of land can be possible.
7) The pest and disease menace for *Kharif* crop will generally be reduced, as their continuous life-cycle breaks by the change of monoculture of rice.

So the cost of cultivation of *Rabi* paddy shown in the preceding page and the cost of cultivation of blackgram is given below, compares the superiority of pulse crop against paddy crop of *Rabi* season.

ALTERNATE PLAN-2: Alternate Farm Plan-2 is presented in Table 8.5.

Table 8.5. Analysis of alternate plan through the use of partial budgeting technique

Cost of cultivation of paddy *(Rabi)*/0.40 ha under Existing Plan

Sl. No.	Operation	Labour		Wages		Total amount (Rs.)
		M	W	M	W	
1.	Land preparation	2	—	24	—	110.00
2.	Nursery raising	2	1	24	10	34.00
3.	F Y M	2	—	24	—	105.00
4.	Seed	2	—	24	—	124.00
5.	Weeding	6	11	72	110	182.00
6.	Fertilisers	2	—	24	—	234.00
7.	Irrigation charges	—	—	—	—	100.00
8.	Harvesting	2	13	24	130	154.00
9.	Plant protection	2	—	24	—	194.00
10.	Land revenue	—	—	—	—	45.00
11.	Interest charges	—	—	—	—	150.00
12.	Others, if any:					
	Threshing	2	2	24	20	44.00
	Drying	2	—	24	—	24.00
					Grand total	1500.00

Table 8.6. Cost of cultivation of blackgram var LBG-17 (0.40 ha)

Sl. No.	Operation	Qty	Amount	Labour		Wages		Total amount (Rs.)
				M	W	M	W	
1.	Land preparation	Tractor hire	80	1	—	24	—	104.00
2.	Seed and sowing	10kg	90	—	3	—	30	120.00
3.	Weeding	—	—	—	18	—	180	180.00
4.	Plant protection: Sulphur W.P. Dithane M-45 Dimethiote	500g 100g 100ml	120	1	—	24	—	144.00
5.	Harvesting	—	—	2	11	24	110	134.00
6.	Fertilisers	—	62	1	—	12	—	74.00
7.	Threshing	—	—	8	4	96	40	136.00
8.	Winnowing & bagging	—	—	3	2	36	20	56.00
						Grand total		948.00

Yield /0.40 ha = 5 qtl = Rate = Rs. 550; Value Rs.2,750
Variety recommended: LBG 17
Value of blackgram/0.40 ha = Rs. 2,750
By-product (fodder)1/2 tonne = Rs. 150
Total returns = Rs. 2,900
Net returns: Rs. 2,900 (–) Rs. 948.00 = Rs. 1952.00 of blackgram
Net returns of *Rabi* paddy: (Rs. 2,830) – (Rs. 1,500)
$$= Rs. 1,330$$
Thus the net returns in production of blackgram is comparatively high with minimum risks.

It is the alternate plan against the existing *Rabi* paddy crop.

ANALYSIS OF ALTERNATE PLAN : THROUGH THE USE OF PARTIAL BUDGETING TECHNIQUE

1) Added costs: Nil
2) Reduced costs: Total reduced cost = Rs. 552
(Rs. 1,500 – Rs. 948)
3) *Added returns*: Since the crop will be grown in alternate plan as blackgram against the *Rabi* paddy of existing plan, the returns are shown in rupees.

Added returns: Rs. 70 only
(Rs. 2,900 (–) Rs. 2,830)
Where returns of blackgram: Rs. 2,900
Returns of paddy   : Rs 2,830
4) Reduced returns: Nil

PROFITABILITY

(Added returns + Reduced cost) – (Reduced returns + Added cost)
(Rs. 70 + Rs. 552) – (0+0)
= Rs. 622/ 0.40 ha
Cost-Benefit Ratio:
Added cost : Added returns
Nil : Rs. 70
So there is no added cost and the entire returns are the benefit only.

PRACTICABILITY OF ALTERNATE PLAN

Cultivation of blackgram is easy, since it is of short duration and involved very little risks. For a paddy farmer it is still easier to cultivate the blackgram.

The short duration of blackgram helps in reducing the duration of crop, which enriches the soil. It also provides the time to grow another crop during summer.

While in paddy cultivation it takes a minimum of four-and-a-half months, as against two to two-and-a-half months for blackgram. So it is highly practicable to grow another green manure-cum-pulse crop in summer.

Index